Affinity Publisher 2.0 For Book Formatting Part 2

AFFINITY PUBLISHER 2.0 FOR
SELF-PUBLISHING - BOOK 2

M.L. HUMPHREY

SELECT TITLES BY M.L. HUMPHREY

AFFINITY PUBLISHER 2.0 FOR SELF-PUBLISHING

AFFINITY PUBLISHER 2.0 FOR BOOK FORMATTING PART 1

AFFINITY PUBLISHER 2.0 FOR BOOK FORMATTING PART 2

AFFINITY PUBLISHER FOR SELF-PUBLISHING

AFFINITY PUBLISHER FOR FICTION LAYOUTS

AFFINITY PUBLISHER FOR AD CREATIVES

AFFINITY PUBLISHER FOR BASIC BOOK COVERS

AFFINITY PUBLISHER FOR NON-FICTION

* * *

DATA ANALYSIS FOR SELF-PUBLISHERS

* * *

EXCEL FOR BEGINNERS

WORD FOR BEGINNERS

POWERPOINT FOR BEGINNERS

ACCESS FOR BEGINNERS

CONTENTS

INTRODUCTION

This book is a continuation of *Affinity Publisher 2.0 for Book Formatting Part 1* which covered how to create a basic black and white print title using master pages, text styles, and a simple accent image. That book also covered how to flow text and export to PDF along with other beginner-level topics.

This book will assume that you already know all of that material and build from there by covering more advanced print-formatting topics, including how to insert a single table of contents, multiple tables of contents, and an index. We'll also cover how to use chapter names instead of the book title in headers or footers, how to have multiple columns of text on a page, how to merge multiple book files into one, and how to insert images into the body of your document.

It is the equivalent of *Affinity Publisher for Non-Fiction*, which was written for the original Affinity Publisher.

If you bought Affinity in late 2022 or later then you probably have version 2.0 and this is the right book for you, but it's best to double-check. You can tell when you open Affinity which version you have because the launch screen for version 2.0 will say Affinity Publisher 2, like in the screenshot below:

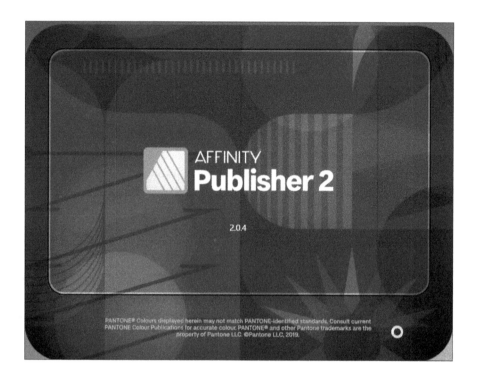

At this point I have formatted over a hundred books in Affinity, but most of those were in the original version of the program, so what I'm doing here is saying, "I know how to do this in the original Affinity program, how does that now work in Affinity Publisher 2.0". Which means that I may not catch all of the new bells and whistles.

But my approach does work and when you finish reading this book you will have a way to do all of the topics listed. I can't promise it's the absolute, most efficient way, but it does work and it works well enough I haven't felt the need to track down a better solution.

Okay. So.

Let's dive in and start with the easiest topic: how to use chapter names instead of the book title for the header or footer. (Again, I'm going to assume you know what was covered in Part I so already have formatted master pages to work with.)

CHAPTER OR SECTION NAMES FOR HEADERS OR FOOTERS

In Part 1 we set up master pages that used the book title in the header. The Text and Text master page looked like this:

Awesome Author	The Best Book Since Sliced Bread
#	#

As mentioned in that book, that title that you see in the top right header in that screenshot is actually the Title field and the text you're seeing there is what we entered for Title in the Fields panel.

But if you want to use chapter or section names instead, then that works a little differently. So first step if you're working from an existing file like we are here, is to delete the existing field from that text frame.

Go to the master page, click on the Artistic Text Tool, click on the text frame that contains the title, Ctrl + A to select the text, delete.

(If you weren't working from an existing file, then create a place for your text to appear like the text frame we have here for the header.)

The next step is to click into the text frame if you haven't already, go to the Text menu option, go down to Insert, then Fields, and then Section Name.

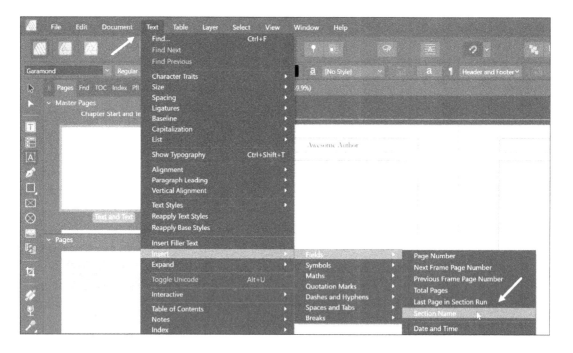

And there you have it:

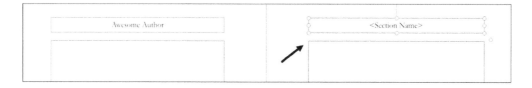

Note that it inserts the field name <Section Name>, because it's going to be different throughout your book depending on the section. (I wish they did the same for the Author and Title fields, but they don't. At least not as of April 2023.)

If you're adapting an existing file, make this change for all of your master pages that use the Title field. For me that's Text and Text and Chapter Start and Text.

Updating the master pages or formatting them to incorporate the Section Name field is step one. Next, you need to give Affinity section names to use. If you were using just the book title before, you're probably going to have a Section Manager that looks like this:

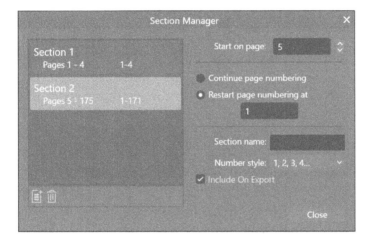

There are only two sections in the document, one for the front matter, one for the main body and backmatter. And the only reason you have two is because you want the start of the first chapter to be numbered page 1.

Note that neither section has a name. The Section Name field is blank and none is listed in the left-hand section listing.

Here, in contrast, is the Section Manager for one of my non-fiction titles:

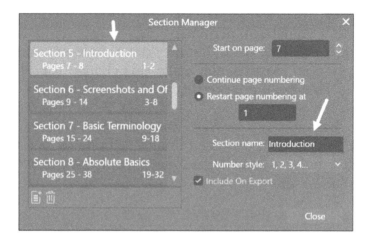

Note that for the selected section, the Section Name field on the right-hand side is now populated (with the text "Introduction") and that a section name is listed for all of the sections in the section listing on the left-hand side of the dialogue box. For example, "Section 5 – Introduction" and "Section 7 – Basic Terminology".

That Section Name field has to be populated for Affinity to use section names.

For each section you will manually input the value, so it does not have to match the chapter name, which is helpful when a chapter name is too long.

It's also helpful for when you want to have a header that spans multiple chapters. For example, when I create an omnibus of my fiction titles, so three of them in one book, I have a section for each novel. The text I use in my header is the title of the novel not the individual chapter names.

Let's go create some sections now to see how this works.

In the Pages section of the Pages panel, find the start point of the first chapter or section that you want to create. Select only the one page of the two-page spread that is the start of the chapter or section. Right-click and choose Start New Section from the dropdown menu.

(If you already created a section that starts on that page, choose Edit Section instead.)

This will open the Section Manager dialogue box. Enter a value for section name and hit Enter. While you have this open, also confirm that the page numbering choice is correct. In general, you're not going to restart your page numbering after the front matter so the "continue page numbering" option should be checked and also the number style will likely be 1, 2, 3, 4.

Click Close.

You'll then need to walk through your document and right-click on the first page of each of your chapters or sections or wherever you want to create a new header, and choose to Start New Section for each one to add it into the Section Manager.

You *can* add a section directly in the Section Manager using the small page with a plus sign icon at the bottom of the section listing, but I don't recommend it. It assigns the page number for the section in a weird way in my opinion. But try it if you want.

You can also edit more than one section at a time with the Section Manager open. Just click onto the section you want to edit on the left-hand side to bring up that section's information and then make your edits. (I sometimes need to do this when I have multiple documents I've merged and need to fix the page numbering settings.)

Every single page in your document must be assigned to a section. Which means that a section will contain all pages from that section forward to the next section you designate. The place to be especially aware of this is at the end of your document. There's the possibility (because I've done it) that you create a section for your last chapter and then forget to create another one for any backmatter and your backmatter ends up using the last chapter's name in the header.

To edit a section name later, just right-click on the thumbnail (or really any thumbnail) in the Pages section of the Pages panel, choose Edit Section, and then go to that section in the Section Manager and change the value for section name.

If you ever need to delete a section you created, that can also be done in the Section Manager by clicking on the section on the left-hand side and then using the trash can below the section listing.

And here we go, a page header that uses section name, in this case for page 3 of Chapter 1 in my document:

To summarize. If you want to use chapter or section names in your document header or footer there are two steps involved. First, make sure your master page is set to use the section field name. Second, create sections and assign them a name.

SINGLE TABLE OF CONTENTS

For simplicity's sake right now, I am going to keep working with the file we created in the prior book in this series, which was a fiction title that used chapter names like Chapter 1, Chapter 2, etc. even though a table of contents is not standard for a novel like that.

Tables of contents are common for short story collections and for non-fiction. I have also seen them used in novels when there are named chapters. And I have used them in novels that included backmatter I wanted a reader to know about, such as a character listing, terminology, or summary of a prior book.

Since I'm using the file from before, the first thing I need is a master page that will work for my table of contents. I copied my Also By master page and edited it to get this:

I made the accent image smaller and moved it to the corner and also moved where the text frame starts higher on the page. For the first page of a table of contents I choose not to include a page number. I named this master page Table of Contents.

Next step is to insert that master page into the document. I'm going to put mine after my also by page, so I go to the Pages section of the Pages panel, right-click on my page spread that includes my also by text, choose to Add Pages, and select 2, After, and Table of Contents for the master page in the Add Pages dialogue box.

Once the new pages are added to my document, I double-click on the thumbnail for those pages, click into the text frame on the right-hand page in my main workspace, and move my cursor to the line below the text that's already there, Table of Contents.

Now we're ready to insert the actual table of contents.

To do that, go to the Table of Contents panel, which we placed in the top left corner in the last book. (If you don't have it, go to Window→References→Table of Contents and that should open it for you.)

This is the top of the panel:

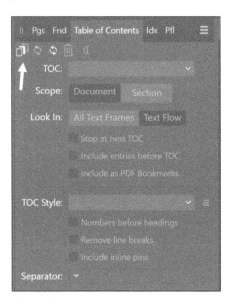

Click on the Insert icon in the top left corner which looks like three pieces of paper stacked on top of one another.

If you used text styles like we did in the last book, chances are this is what you'll get:

That is because by default Affinity is going to use Heading 1 and Heading 2 text styles to drive the table of contents entries. You can see that in the bottom of the Table of Contents panel where those two boxes are checked:

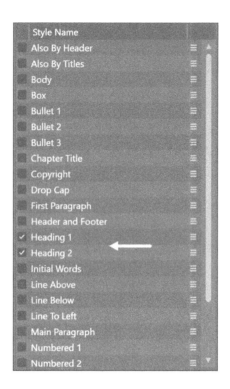

Uncheck those boxes and check the box for the text style or styles that you used to create your chapter or section headers. In my case, that is going to be Chapter Title. As soon as I did that, the table of contents turned into this:

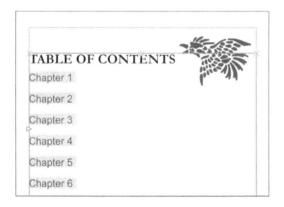

Better. But I also want page numbering. To include page numbers, go back to the Style Name section of the Table of Contents panel and click on the three lines at the end of the row for each style you want to use. In the dialogue box that appears, check the box for Include Page Number:

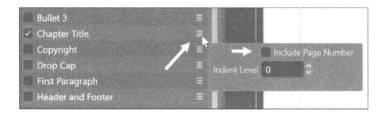

Now I have this:

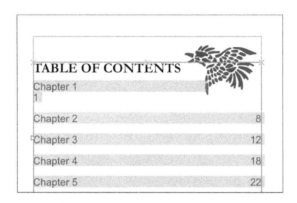

You can see I have page numbers now, but I also have an issue because my image that I included on the page dips down enough to make the page number for the first chapter wrap to the next line. I need to go back to the master page and do one of two things. I can either move the start of the text frame down a bit so that doesn't happen, or I can change the Text Wrap Settings related to that image so that any text that overlaps the image jumps the image. (I could also just delete the image and then center the header.)

In this case, I'm just going to change where the text starts.

But I have another issue. The default text formatting for table of contents entries uses Arial 12 point and the rest of my document is using Garamond.

If you click on a text entry in the table of contents, you'll see that Affinity assigns a text style to TOC entries. In this case it's calling the style TOC 1: Chapter Title since this is the first table of contents in the document and the text style that's feeding into these entries is the Chapter Title.

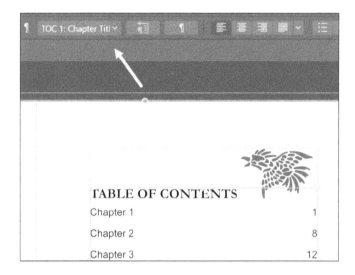

Each text style that feeds into your table of contents will have its own assigned text style. So if you use two different text styles to populate your table of contents and want to reformat the entries, you'll need to do this twice.

Take one of the entries in the table of contents and change the formatting to what you want to use, in my case Garamond 12 pt. I will often also, for non-fiction, use the Typography section of the Character panel to make my entries small caps or all caps as well.

Click on Update Paragraph Style to apply that change to the text style. (As a reminder the update option is in the dynamic menu up top and to the right of the dropdown that shows the text style name.)

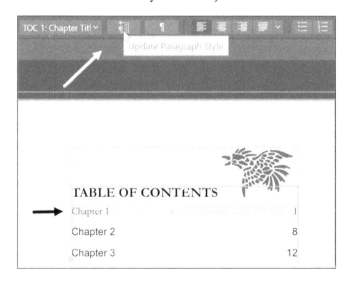

That should automatically update all of your TOC entries that use that style. But this one is sometimes finicky.

For example, for me just now it didn't update all of my entries. It updated the page numbering, but not the text side of the entry. And even when I just highlighted the text for a chapter entry and did it again, it still failed to work. But unchecking and rechecking the box for Chapter Title in the Table of Contents panel fixed it. Of course, I then had to tell it to use page numbers again because it reverted back to the original settings.

So if something doesn't work immediately, play around with it a bit. It may be the program not you.

It is possible to just manually format your text in your table of contents. You could select all of the text in the table, format it to your heart's content, and do it that way. But the problem is, that you can never ever again update that table of contents. Because as soon as you refresh the table, Affinity will go back to the assigned text style for those entries which is in Arial 12 point.

This is also why you should never fix a typo or anything like that directly in the table of contents. Go find the entry in the document that has the typo and fix it there. Everything you see in your table of contents is auto-generated and populated by Affinity and so can be overwritten. Which means, ideally, you insert that table of contents and never touch anything in it after it's inserted.

(With the exception of changing the formatting and then saving that as the TOC formatting, of course.)

Let's say you did have a typo. Here we are, I just looked at this list and Chapter is misspelled for Chapter 1:

The way to fix this is to go to Chapter 1 and change it there. Next, go to the Table of Contents panel, click on the text frame that contains the table of contents so that you can see the options for it, and click on either Update or Update All Table of Contents at the top of the panel:

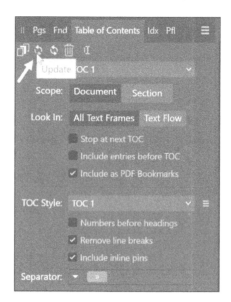

In this case, both options will do the same thing and update this table of contents.

You can also, go to Preflight and click on the Fix button next to "One or more tables of contents entries need updating":

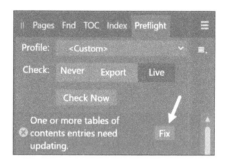

If you ever manually update your table of contents, Preflight is going to tell you that your table of contents entries need updating. So be very careful if that's how you choose to handle an issue. It can be easy to forget, click on Fix in Preflight, and then break whatever it was that you manually changed.

If you have a lot of table of contents entries, like I do here, they will require more than one page and you will see that the text frame is overflowing. In that case, you will need to create and insert another master page to handle that and then manually flow the text from this page to that one.

Let's do that in the next chapter as part of showing you how to have two types of page numbering in a document.

USE TWO TYPES OF PAGE NUMBERING

The front matter in a book, which is everything that falls before the main text of the book is supposed to use a different page numbering than the main book. The front matter uses small Roman numerals (i, ii, iii, iv, etc.) whereas the main part of the book uses the more traditional 1, 2, 3, etc. Backmatter, if numbered, usually continues with the main body numbering.

Now, it turns out that the way I have handled page numbering for front matter in the past is wrong. When I include it, I just start the numbering with my table of contents so that page two or three of my table of contents is numbered ii or iii.

But, I just took a gander at a bunch of books on my shelf and when they number the pages they treat the entire front matter as the same. So that the second or third page of a table of contents ends up being page x or page viii or wherever it happens to fall in those first pages, even if none of the other pages in the front matter are numbered.

Good news is that if you keep your table of contents short you can avoid this headache altogether because none of the books I checked used a page number if the table of contents fit on the first page. Many also didn't use page numbering if the table of contents was only two pages long.

But let's say you do want to number that second page in the table of contents. Or maybe you have an Introduction to a classic novel that you want to treat as front matter and it needs to be numbered differently.

Easy enough to do.

First, make sure that your master pages are set up to display page numbering for that part of the book. If it was the table of contents, you'd have the first page not show a page number, but any subsequent pages show it, for example.

Second, go to the Pages section of the Pages panel and right-click on one of the thumbnails to choose Edit Section and bring up the Section Manager:

Chances are Section 1 will be your front matter. Use the Number Style dropdown for that section to change the numbering style to lower-case Roman numerals:

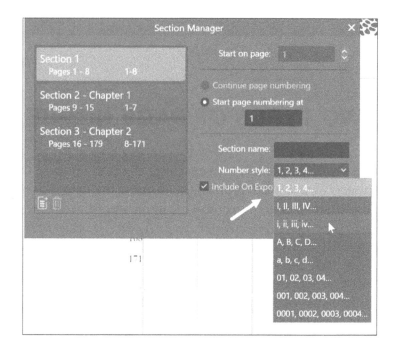

That will ensure that any of the pages in your front matter that use a page number in their layout include the appropriate value.

Your next section should already be set up, but if it isn't make sure it uses the 1, 2, 3, 4, etc. numbering style and is set to restart at 1.

And here we go:

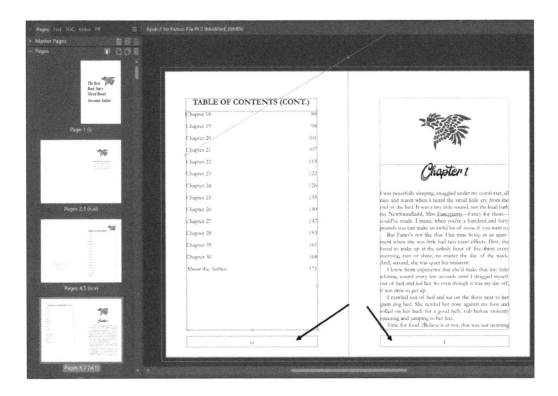

I moved the copyright notice around since I have a table of contents now, which means my front matter ends with the last page of my table of contents. You can see here that that last page of my front matter is page vi and then the main text starts on the next page with page 1.

Personally, even though I know it's wrong, I still prefer to just number my table of contents pages and not all of my front matter. If you want to do that, then you need to create a new section for the table of contents and tell Affinity to restart numbering for that section in addition to setting the number style to lower-case Roman numerals. However, keep in mind that you shouldn't do that if you have more than one element in your front matter that needs to be numbered.

COLUMNS

We'll circle back to tables of contents again later and discuss how to have more than one in your document, but first I want to cover a couple other topics, namely indexes and how to have multiple columns of text on the page.

When I insert an index into the back of my non-fiction books I use two columns per page, because a short entry like that doesn't need its own dedicated line. Here for example is the first page of the index from one of my Word 365 books:

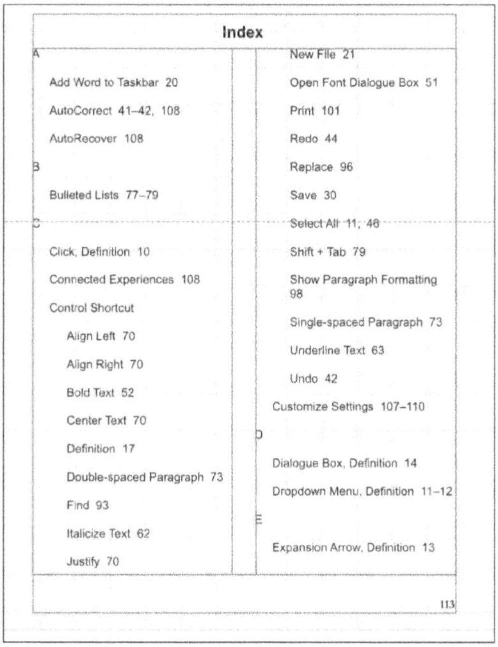

Index

A

Add Word to Taskbar 20	New File 21
AutoCorrect 41–42, 108	Open Font Dialogue Box 51
AutoRecover 108	Print 101
	Redo 44
B	Replace 96
Bulleted Lists 77–79	Save 30
C	Select All 11, 46
Click, Definition 10	Shift + Tab 79
Connected Experiences 108	Show Paragraph Formatting 98
Control Shortcut	Single-spaced Paragraph 73
Align Left 70	Underline Text 63
Align Right 70	Undo 42
Bold Text 52	Customize Settings 107–110
Center Text 70	D
Definition 17	Dialogue Box, Definition 14
Double-spaced Paragraph 73	Dropdown Menu, Definition 11–12
Find 93	E
Italicize Text 62	Expansion Arrow, Definition 13
Justify 70	

113

You can see that using two columns works just fine for an index like this. So let's go set up a master page for this and I'll show you how to have multiple columns on a page.

I'm just going to copy the master page for Text and Text and then convert the right-hand page to an index page. So, go to the Master Pages section of the Pages panel, right-click on the Text and Text thumbnail, Duplicate, rename, drag to the end, double-click on the thumbnail.

I want page numbering, so we can leave that, but I'm going to shorten the text frame in the main text area and drag down what is now a header and turn it into an Index label at the top of that space using my Chapter Title Header text style to replace the text currently in that field.

I also removed the text flow between the two text frames. Here we are:

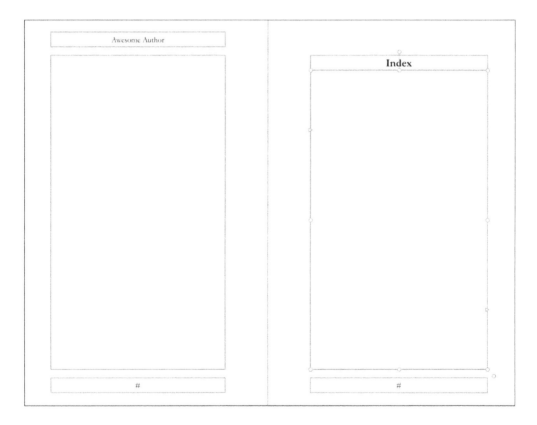

Click on the Move Tool if you don't already have it selected (the black arrow) and then click on the main text frame on the index page.

On the far right of the dynamic menu up top there should be a Columns option. If it isn't visible, it's because of how big your screen is or how much you have your screen zoomed in. Click on the double-arrow at the end of the row to see the columns option.

Here, for me, for example, the gutter width setting for columns is not immediately visible:

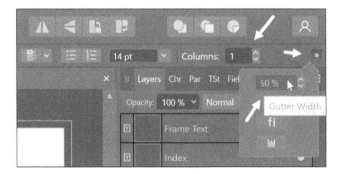

You can also open the Text Frame panel, which is under Window→Text→Text Frame. The second section of that panel is for Columns settings and the third is for Column Rules. I've minimized General here and expanded those two sections so you can see the available options:

When you choose to have multiple columns, Affinity will by default preserve the width of the text frame and will apply a .333 inch gutter between them.

Here, for example, I have a text frame that is 3.75 inches wide. Choosing two columns creates columns that are each 1.708 inches wide:

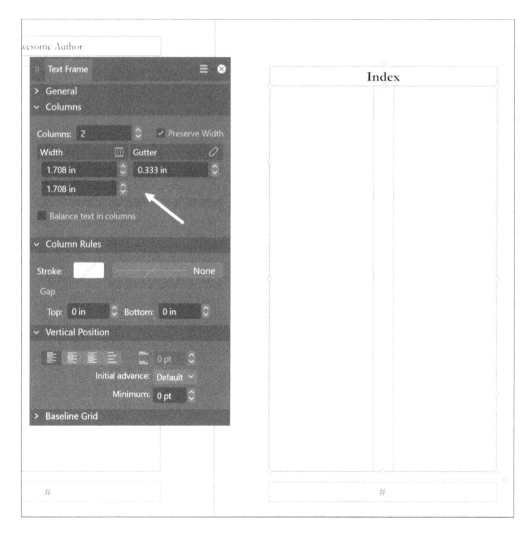

If I ask for three columns, it defaults to 1.028 inches for each column with .333 inch gutters between them:

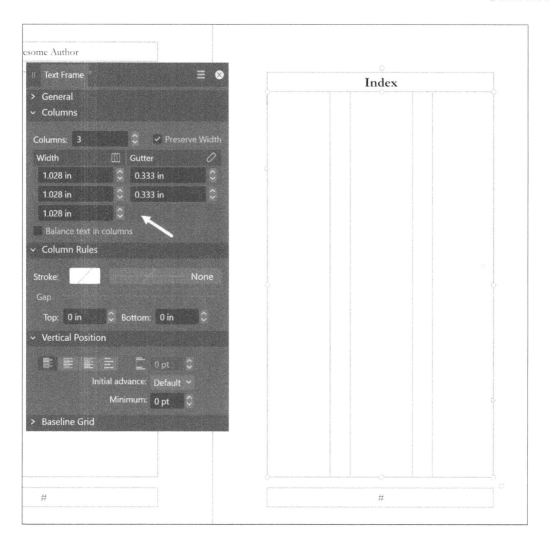

You can edit those values and Affinity will adjust. Here, for example, I changed one of the gutters to .125 inches and it changed my column widths to 1.167 inches and the other gutter value to .125 inches:

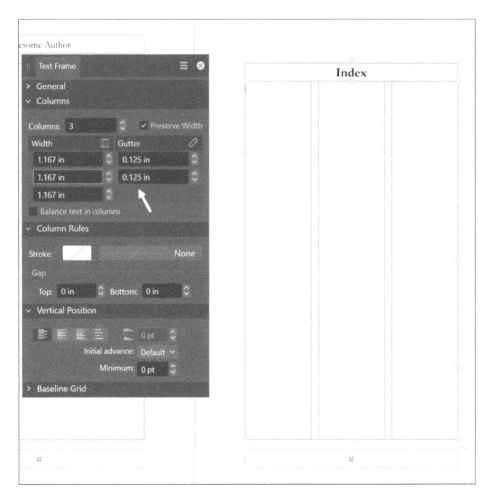

Keep in mind that the blue lines you see right now in that text frame will not exist on the printed page. So it will just be text in three columns with that space between them.

It is possible to add a line in the gutter between your columns. That's in the Column Rules section of the Text Frame panel.

Click on the white box next to Stroke. It will say Column Rule Stroke Fill if you hold your mouse over it:

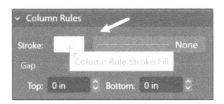

When you click on that box a pop-up dialogue box will appear that lets you choose the color of the line that you're going to place between the columns. It looks like it defaults to the Color tab, but for what we're doing here which is black and white, we can click over to the Swatches tab and choose the black swatch:

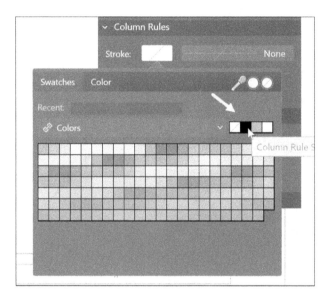

By default Affinity will use a line that is .2 pt wide:

Click on the line in the Text Frame panel to bring up a pop-up dialogue box that allows you to specify the line width and style. By default it is a solid line, but you can also have a dotted line by clicking on the dotted line image in the style row. To change the line thickness either click into the field and type a value or click and drag the white button along the Width line:

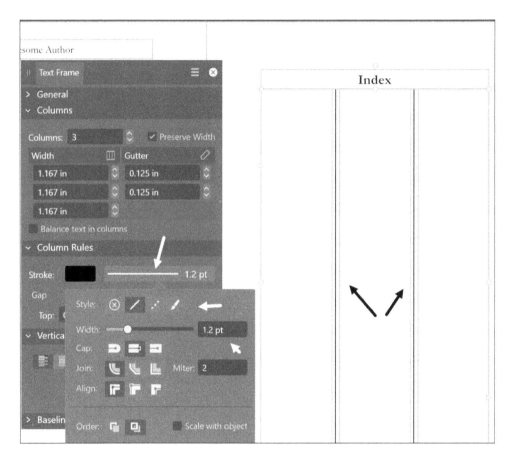

Above I've kept the line solid but made it 1.2 pt wide which is much more obvious.

If you want the lines to have a shape, like an arrow, at the ends, that is under Start and End. Here is the dropdown menu that shows all those available choices:

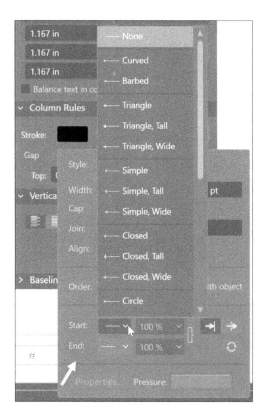

You can also set the line so that it doesn't start at the very top or end at the very bottom by changing the Top and Bottom values in the Column Rules section of the Text Frame panel. Here I've set the lines to start half an inch below the top of the frame and to end a half an inch above the bottom of the frame:

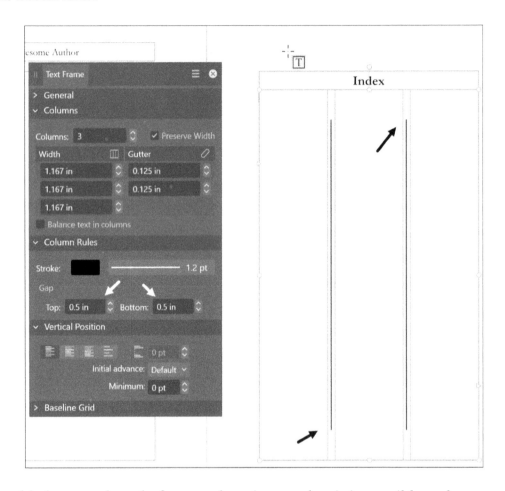

I should also note here before we drop in text that it is possible to have uneven columns by changing the Width values in the Columns section of the Text Frame panel, but I wouldn't recommend it because the text is going to flow from one column straight to the next. If you're looking for uneven columns, chances are what you're trying to do is probably more of a two-column text frame next to a standalone narrow text frame that contains pull-out quotes or something like that.

But it is possible to do. Affinity will auto-adjust the width of the next column to keep the total text frame width the same unless you uncheck that "preserve width" box.

Okay. Text time. I'm going to go back to two columns for this.

But first I'm going to remove that line between the columns. To do that, click on the rectangle next to Stroke in the Column Rules section of the Text Frame panel and click on the "no color" option which is a white circle with a red line across it.

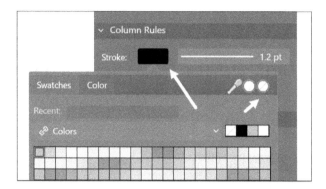

I want to add my text in the actual document, not the master page, so I need to go to the Pages section, add pages, add this master page style, and then I can drop in some text.

I want to ultimately use this for an index, but there's something else I want to show you with columns that is best seen with regular text, so I have dropped in part of the last chapter of a book here so you can see the text flow:

Index

Fortunately for me, once Mark Fletcher heard that Don was dead, he told the cops all about what had happened. I was right, Don had killed Janice Fletcher to hasten Mark's inheritance. Seems Mark had talked a good talk about how rich his family was to get Don's boss to extend him a very generous line of credit, one that wasn't going to be paid off by the little plot of land he'd inherited. When Don learned that the money had all gone to the cats, he took his frustrations out on Mark. If we hadn't stopped him then, the next victim might have been Patsy Blackstone and who knows who else, because the list of people designated as cat caretakers before Mark Fletcher was a very long one indeed.

We learned all of the details at Taco Tuesday that next week.

Matt was there. So was Mason. And Jamie.

I watched Mason and Jamie laughing and talking back and forth and decided that maybe Mason wasn't such a bad choice for my friend after all. He had risked his life for her. Would Lucas Dean have done the same? I think not.

By default, the text is going to completely fill the first column and then move on to the top of the next column as you can see above. If you want the text to be evenly balanced between the two columns, you need to check the Balance Text In Columns field in the Columns section of the Text Frame panel. That will give the text this type of appearance instead:

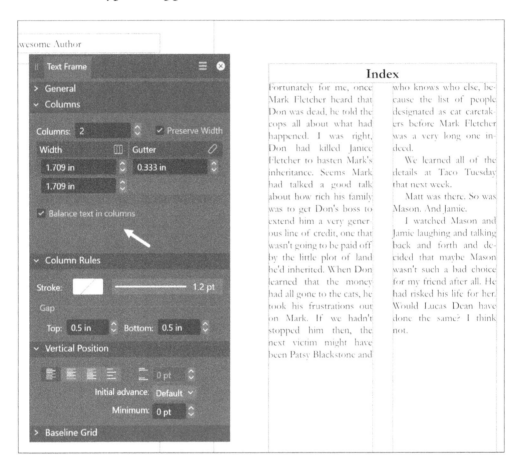

It is also possible to force text into the next column using a Column Break. Click where you want to break the text and then go to Text→Insert→Breaks→Column Break:

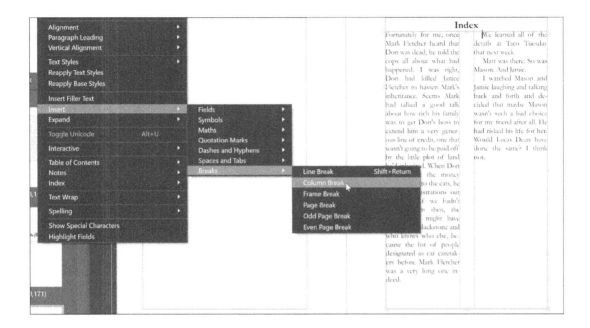

We're going to now use this for an index instead of basic text. So let's clear out that text and now learn how to insert an index.

INDEXES

An index lets you create a listing, generally at the back of your book, of where key subjects are discussed within the main body of the document. As far as I know, you only get one index per book. (Unlike tables of contents where you can have more than one throughout the book.)

I use these for most of my non-fiction titles, but because we already started Part 1 with a fiction title, I'm just going to go with that to show how this works.

I had an issue early on with my index entries in the original version of Affinity Publisher where I would try to flag an entry as an index entry and instead end up inserting an index at that point in my document, and when I tried to undo that it would crash Affinity. So that drives part of how I approach inserting an index in Affinity.

It may not be an issue anymore. But I don't think it hurts to do things this way either.

Okay. So what I do is find an entry towards the back of my book and mark it as an index entry.

MARK AN INDEX ENTRY

To do this, click on the Artistic Text Tool, select the text that you want to flag, go to the Index panel, and click on Insert Marker.

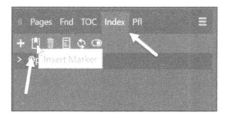

It should, and it did for me just now, bring up an Insert Index Mark dialogue box that contains that selected text as your Topic Name. Change the text if you need to, and then click on OK.

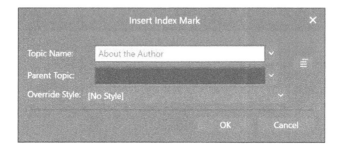

Sometimes in the past it would not include the text for me if I did this through the Index Panel, so you may have to manually type it in yourself, but hopefully that issue has been fixed in 2.0.

Your other option would be to go to Text→Index→Insert Index Mark or use Ctrl + Alt + Shift + [to insert an index mark. (I personally never use that control shortcut because it's just too much for me to remember each time.)

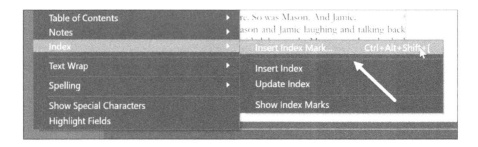

Note in the image above how Insert Index is right below Insert Index Mark? This is where I'd get myself in trouble, because I'd accidentally select Insert Index instead of Insert Index Mark.

To prevent that possibility, once you have a single index mark, go to where you want to place your index in your document, and insert it. Since you can only have one index in a document that will prevent you from accidentally inserting an index elsewhere.

INSERT AN INDEX

To insert an index in your document, click into the text frame where you want the index, and then go to the Index panel and click on the option for Insert Index at the top. It should be the fourth icon you see:

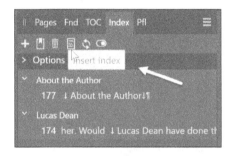

(You could also use the menu option I pointed out above.)

Affinity will insert an index into your document at that location. Like so:

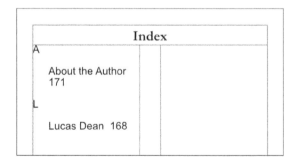

I only have two entries so far, so that's what you can see here.

Next, walk through the rest of your document, find text entries you want to add to your index, and create markers from them.

UPDATE INDEX

If you are lucky, the index will update automatically as you add new entries. For the last half dozen books I did, that's what happened for me. But just now while working on this index here, it didn't.

If your index does not automatically update as you add new entries, simply use the Update Index option at the top of the Index panel (the little arrows in a circle) to update the contents of the index.

I don't really worry about it either way until I've flagged all of my entries. At which point you'll either get to the end and have a page or more of entries listed, or you'll get to the end and have that one single entry you started with.

If it's just the one, refresh. If they're all there, great, you don't have to do anything else.

I have yet to see a pattern as to when it works and when it doesn't. For me, the index is one of the less stable areas of Affinity Publisher.

SEE INDEX MARKS

The other item at the end of that top menu in the Index panel is a little toggle that lets you turn on and off index marks in your document. I usually keep that turned off, but if you weren't sure something had been flagged yet, you could turn that on to see.

It's very subtle. It's a light-gray-colored flag which you can (perhaps) see on the last line of this paragraph:

I watched Mason and Jamie laughing and talking back and forth and decided that maybe Mason wasn't such a bad choice for my friend after all. He had risked his life for her. Would Lucas Dean have done the same? I think not.

ADD TOPIC

Your other option at the top of the Index panel is on the far left and is a small plus sign. That lets you add a topic without adding an index marker. Click on it to bring up the Add Index Topic dialogue box:

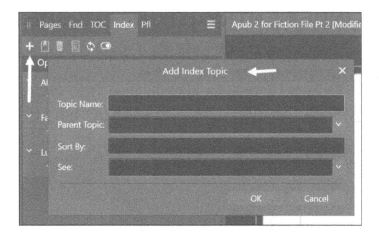

I sometimes use this for topics like "Definitions" that aren't going to be directly-flagged entries. I can then flag individual entries such as Dialogue Box, Dropdown Menu, etc. and assign Definitions as the parent topic, which puts those individual entries as sub-topics under that heading.

Here, for example, I added "Characters" as a topic:

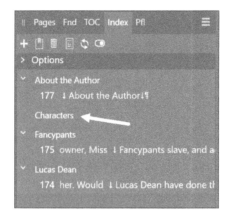

You can see that it has no flagged entries because there's no page number and text listed below it like for the other three.

MOVE INDEX ENTRY TO CREATE SUBTOPIC

If you want to move existing entries to be a sub-topic of another existing entry, you can left-click on the entry and drag to do so.

Here I left-clicked on Fancypants and dragged it to under the Characters topic. Now Fancypants is indented and shown as a sub-topic of Characters.

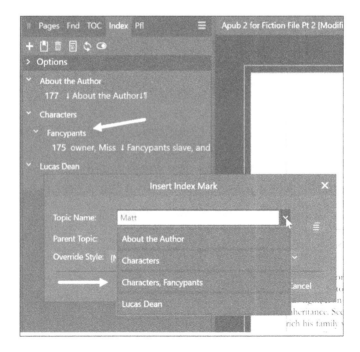

I also have the Insert Index Mark dialogue box showing here so you can see that Fancypants is now listed as "Characters, Fancypants". The first text listed is the highest level for the entry and then there's a comma and then the sub-entry text.

INSERT NEW ENTRY AS SUBTOPIC

For a new entry that you want to insert as a sub-topic, choose the topic name like you would for any other index entry, but then also use the Parent Topic dropdown menu to choose the associated main topic:

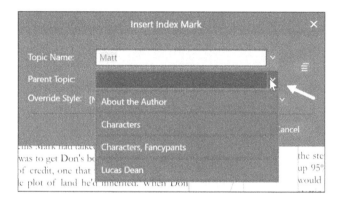

EDIT EXISTING ENTRY TO CREATE SUBTOPIC

Another way to assign a topic as a sub-topic is to right-click on the topic once it's listed in your index entries listing and choose to Edit Topic:

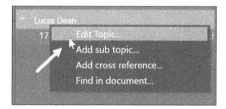

This will bring up the Edit Index Topic dialogue box which allows you to select a Parent Topic, like I did here with Characters:

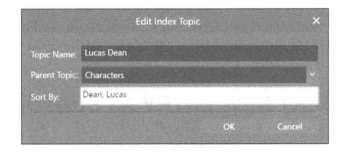

MOVE A SUBTOPIC TO PARENT TOPIC LEVEL

To move a subtopic up to its own level, right-click, choose to Edit Topic, and then delete the parent topic information and click on OK.

EDIT EXISTING ENTRY

You can also use the Edit Topic dialogue box to change the text for the Topic Name if needed.

Another option is to click on the name itself in the Index panel and edit it directly, but if you do so it will overwrite the whole name and you will have to type it all in from scratch.

CHANGE SORT ORDER FOR INDEX ENTRY

In the above image of the Edit Index Topic dialogue box you can see that in the Sort By field I typed in "Dean, Lucas". If you type a value into that field, Affinity will sort that index entry based upon the text in the Sort By field instead of the text in the Topic Name field.

In general you would use this for a situation where the Topic Name includes a word at the start like "the" that you didn't want to drive the sort order.

But you can see here that it worked in this instance as well because "Lucas Dean" is now sorted above "Fancypants":

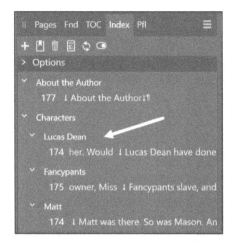

INSERT ANOTHER MARKER FOR THE SAME TOPIC

If you already have one entry for a topic, click anywhere on the word and click to insert a marker and you should see something like this where it selected the whole word and then suggested any existing topics that match that text:

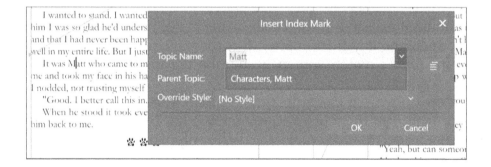

Click on that entry and the parent and topic name will all populate.

ASSIGN AN INDEX TOPIC TO A PAGE RANGE

If you want Affinity to list an index entry for a page range, flag each page in that range for that topic even if that word is not specifically used on that page. Just click somewhere on the page and insert a marker and then choose the marker you want from the dropdown menu.

Affinity will show a page range when you have two or more pages in a row flagged, like I did here:

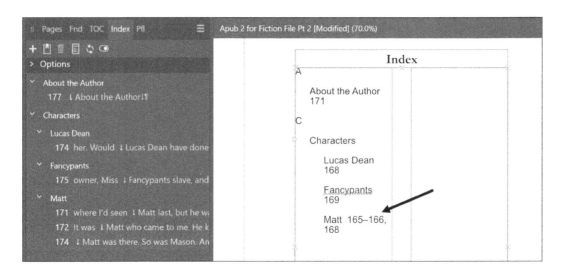

PAGE NUMBERS USED IN YOUR INDEX

Look at the page numbers in the image above.

The page number listed in the Index panel is the page number for the entire document, including any front matter. But the page number that is displayed in the actual index will match your page numbering in your document. So most likely the two will not match.

You can see above, for example, that "Lucas Dean" was flagged on page 174 of the document. But the index shows that as page 168 because that is the page number that a reader would actually see if they flipped through the book looking for that entry.

DELETE INDEX ENTRY

To delete an entry that you have listed for the index, just click on it and then click on the trash can at the top of the Index panel.

CROSS-REFERENCES

To create a cross-reference, for a new topic add that information in the See field: It will look like this:

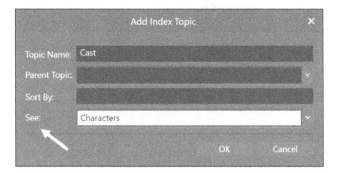

If it's an existing topic, right-click and choose Add Cross Reference, and then

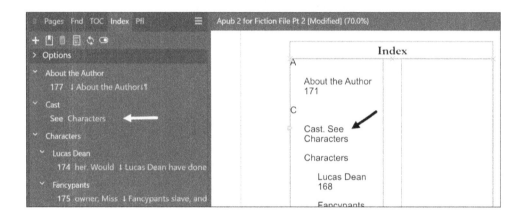

choose in the dropdown the topic to cross reference to.

FIND ALL INSTANCES OF INDEXED TERM IN DOCUMENT

Once you've added a topic, you can right-click on that topic and choose Find in Document from the dropdown. That will show you all instances of that word in the document:

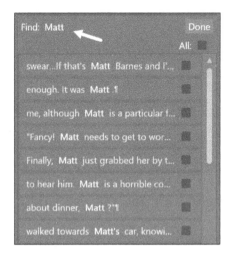

You can see the text around each usage if you're not sure you want to include an entry. Click on one of the entries to be taken to that page in the document and see the full text surrounding the use of the term.

ADD ALL INSTANCES OF INDEXED TERM TO INDEX

After searching for an indexed term, if you click the All box at top, all of those instances will be added as index entries for that topic. You can also check the individual boxes next to each entry to choose which ones to include.

Click Done when you're finished selecting which entries to include to return to the main view in the Index panel.

MANUAL CHANGES TO YOUR INDEX

Once you've inserted an index into your document it is possible to manually change that index and I have done so on occasion.

The default is for each letter of the alphabet that has an entry to display separately. So you can see here, for example, that M and N each only have one entry and display separately:

But at times that has pushed my index off to the next page in ways that I didn't like. Maybe I only had one entry on the last page. Or maybe the S category fell so that the S was on one page but all of its entries were on the next.

In those cases, I have manually combined the M and N categories to bring the text up.

But you have to be careful if you ever do that, because Affinity will overwrite that change if the index is updated after that point and Preflight will tell you that the index needs updated. So if you do a manual change like that, make it the last thing you ever do in that file.

Also, any spelling issues, etc. should not be fixed manually. Make those in the Index panel on that specific entry not in the index that you placed in your document.

TEXT STYLES

The index uses text styles so you can edit your entries to use your chosen font, etc. and then update that text style to carry that through all entries in the index.

Each level of the index uses a different text style, so requires separate formatting if you're going to change the font or other attributes from the default.

But this does allow you to have different formatting (like italics) on your sub-topics or sub-sub-topics.

MERGING MULTIPLE DOCUMENTS WITH INDEX ENTRIES

When you merge multiple documents that used an index, all of those markers will feed into the one document index so you will not have to redo all of that work. (Yay. Because creating an index for a two-hundred page non-fiction book can be hours of work.)

REUSING A FILE THAT HAD AN INDEX

If you ever reuse a file that had an index, be sure to go to the Index panel and see if there are still entries listed there. It is very likely you will have to select and delete them manually even if you've already deleted the pages of your document that had those entries or included the index.

I have found in the past that I also needed to do this a handful of entries at a time. It wouldn't let me delete all of my index entries at once. So I had to use Shift and click to select a range of entries and then use the trash can and keep doing that until they were all gone.

* * *

One final note on indexes. As I mentioned above, indexes have been the most glitchy part of Affinity for me. This is where Affinity is most likely to crash. Or where things just don't quite work the way they should. So I just want to encourage you to breathe deeply if you work with them and accept that things may not go smoothly. But trust me that using the Index panel is far better than trying to manually build an index yourself.

And, also, they seem to be constantly improving the product, so things are bound to get better. (Fingers-crossed.) Okay, on to images.

IMAGES

Alright. Now we're up to a key non-fiction topic, at least for the types of books I write, but one that may not be as relevant for those who write fiction, and that is placing images directly into your text.

If you're reading this book in print, you'll see probably a hundred examples of that in one book. I like to keep things simple so I have the text jump my images. That means I put an image on its own line. You don't have to do that. You can have text wrap around an image instead. And it may very well look better to do so, it just probably requires more time per image if you take that approach.

So. Let's get some images into our book and see how this all works. In Part 1 we had an accent image we used that was inserted directly onto a master page.

But what I've found works best for my books is to use a picture frame and bring my pictures into that frame instead. I'm going to show you a couple other options first, though.

Let's get a Text and Text page spread to work with. I went ahead and used Text→Insert Filler Text to get enough nice Latin gibberish for both frames. But I then had to copy that, paste it into Word, and then bring it back and paste it into Affinity to let it be editable. I also had to go to Text→Spelling→Check Spelling While Typing to turn off the spellcheck that had put a red squiggly line under every word.

But here we are, two text frames full of text:

Etiam ac augue. Morbi tincidunt neque ut lacus. Duis vulputate cursus orci. Mauris justo lorem, scelerisque sit amet, placerat sed, condimentum in, leo. Donec urna est, semper quis, auctor eget, ultrices in, purus. Etiam rutrum. Aliquam blandit dui a libero. Praesent tortor tortor, bibendum vehicula, accumsan sed, adipiscing a, pede. Nullam et tortor. Suspendisse tempor leo quis nunc fringilla volutpat. Donec rutrum ullamcorper lorem. Nunc tincidunt sagittis augue. Quisque lacinia. Phasellus sollicitudin.

Mauris purus. Donec est nunc, ornare non, aliquet non, tempus vel, dolor. Integer sapien nibh, egestas ut, cursus sit amet, faucibus a, sapien. Vestibulum purus purus, elementum ac, luctus ullamcorper, ornare vitae, massa. Nullam posuere sem ut mauris. Nullam velit. Quisque sodales. Donec suscipit suscipit erat. Nam blandit. Praesent congue lorem non dolor. Maecenas vitae erat. Ut ac purus vel purus dapibus gravida.

Nullam lorem sapien, tempus ac, fringilla at, elementum sed, purus. Duis molestie pede. Vivamus quis odio sit amet libero sodales tincidunt. Nam sit amet metus vitae lectus ullamcorper dignissim. Suspendisse leo. Praesent turpis justo, aliquet ac, accumsan vel, posuere quis, pede. Morbi pretium lacus. Cras non metus. Donec laoreet sem at elit. Cum sociis natoque penatibus et magnis dis parturient montes, nascetur ridiculus mus. Vivamus iaculis dolor id felis. Phasellus cursus nulla non odio. Nulla a lectus sed nisi luctus pretium. Sed egestas rutrum odio. Nunc ornare arcu. Quisque at augue ac magna sollicitudin sodales. Donec nulla justo, adipiscing sit amet, feugiat ac, facilisis euismod, risus.

Pellentesque tincidunt, dolor eu dignissim mollis, justo sapien iaculis pede, vel tincidunt lacus nisl sit amet metus. Fusce ac est vitae purus varius tristique. Phasellus mattis ornare ligula. Donec id nibh. Vestibulum metus quam, ultrices in, sagittis tincidunt, gravida et, sapien. Sed

bibendum, lectus vitae tincidunt dapibus, sem felis posuere est, id ornare augue lorem in purus. Suspendisse ligula. Sed mollis tristique mauris. Nullam nunc nunc, aliquet et, tristique nec, porttitor quis, urna. Etiam eu erat. Morbi ut nisl. Curabitur semper sem. Nulla turpis nibh, tempor nec, aliquet vitae, elementum ac, mauris.

Quisque pellentesque metus ac quam. Donec magna nulla, aliquet vitae, congue ac, faucibus ut, erat. Donec sit amet neque. Donec posuere tempus massa. Duis vulputate mauris sit amet purus. Duis vestibulum. Fusce ac erat. Curabitur sagittis. Pellentesque ultricies, ante id lobortis feugiat, ipsum magna congue risus, pulvinar euismod arcu nunc ac turpis. Cum sociis natoque penatibus et magnis dis parturient montes, nascetur ridiculus mus. Aliquam vel quam ut tellus gravida faucibus. Vivamus justo est, elementum vitae, malesuada eu, fermentum in, sapien. Donec sit amet justo. In velit. Vivamus turpis pede, dignissim sed, scelerisque nec, pretium sit amet, dui. Nam nec felis non turpis hendrerit varius. In ultrices ornare lorem. Quisque bibendum, massa sed venenatis malesuada, diam ipsum blandit urna, vel ultricies pede nulla vitae lacus.

Lorem ipsum dolor sit amet, consectetuer adipiscing elit. Quisque in augue. Donec aliquam magna nonummy enim. Proin blandit imperdiet sem. Donec malesuada, urna sit amet varius aliquam, nibh tortor laoreet turpis, eget sodales felis nibh ac sapien. Fusce eget augue. Integer sed risus. Aenean mollis. Donec facilisis egestas quam. Duis bibendum augue id mauris. Sed laoreet, tortor vel cursus fringilla, turpis elit vestibulum arcu, eu varius dolor leo in nulla. In sem ipsum, faucibus quis, varius tristique, porta eget, lorem. Curabitur hendrerit diam et mauris. Etiam porta nunc euismod dui. Maecenas a lectus. In hac habitasse platea dictumst. Suspendisse id massa. Nullam porta velit sed lacus. Duis eleifend, felis eu euismod lacinia, felis erat feugiat nisl, vitae congue leo velit a massa. Quisque nec justo a turpis posuere tristique.

I can now click at the beginning of that second paragraph and use the Place Image Tool to place an image. If I do so, this is what happens:

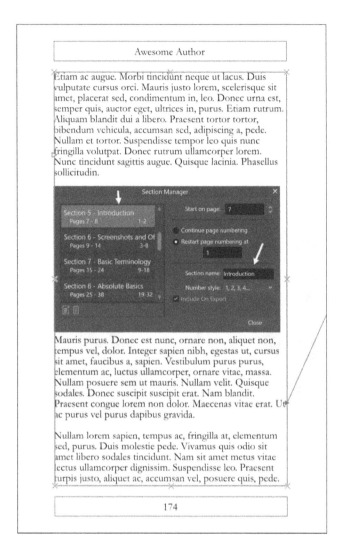

That screenshot of the Section Manager dialogue box inserted into my document at that point and at a size that made its resolution 300 DPI, which is the DPI I have specified for this document.

Here is another image inserted into the document at the same point using the Place Image Tool:

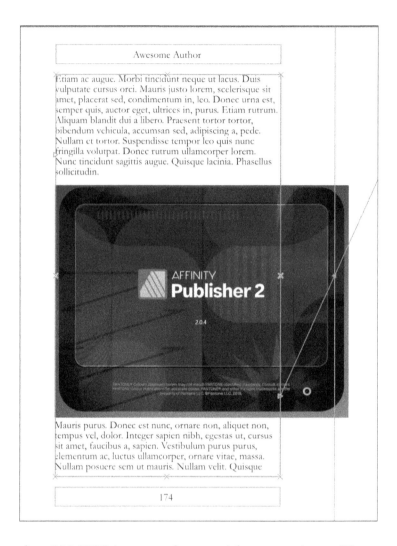

It also inserted at 300 DPI in accordance with my settings. (To see your DPI for your document, at least on a PC, go to File→Document Setup→Document and look at the specified DPI value.)

If you make that image smaller than it is right now, the DPI will go up. Make it larger, the DPI will go down. So that image as inserted into my document is as large as I can use, because for print you need a minimum DPI of 300.

(If you're ever struggling to get a higher DPI on your inserted images, chances are that you need a better display resolution to capture better images. Trying to fix it at this point is generally going to be too late in the process.)

You can see the DPI of an image in your document in one of two ways. Click on the Move Tool (the black arrow) and then click on the image layer in the

Layers panel. In the dynamic menu up top it will show the image name as well as its dimensions and DPI.

This image is 1468x1125 pixels and 300 DPI.

Your other option is to go to Window→Resource Manager. That will list all images in your document at once. Scroll to the right to see the placed DPI for each image:

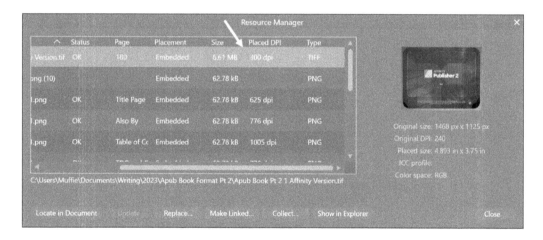

If you don't see a value there, like we don't for the second line, it's because the image is embedded in the document and used more than once. Expand that listing to see each usage and its corresponding DPI value.

The Resource Manager is the quick and easy way to see if any of the images in your document are below the minimum. Since my images come in at 300 DPI I generally don't have to worry about DPI as long as I only make images smaller and don't try to make them larger.

The two images above imported inline with the text. The good thing about an image that is inline with text (or pinned, which we'll discuss in a moment) is that it will move with the text.

Here I've inserted a different image at that same point and then changed my master page to Chapter Start and Text:

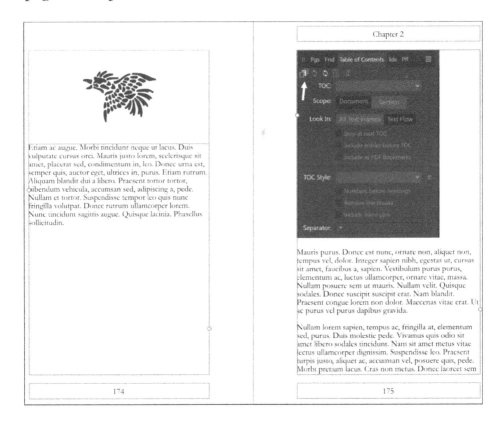

When the different formatting of the master page moved the text down, it took the image with it.

An image inserted inline into text acts like another line of text in the document and will move just like any line of text would.

In this case, the image is tall enough it had to move to the next page because there was no longer enough room for it on the first page. And because it's inline it has to fit in our text frame. I could make it smaller and it would move back to the first page, automatically.

Here we go:

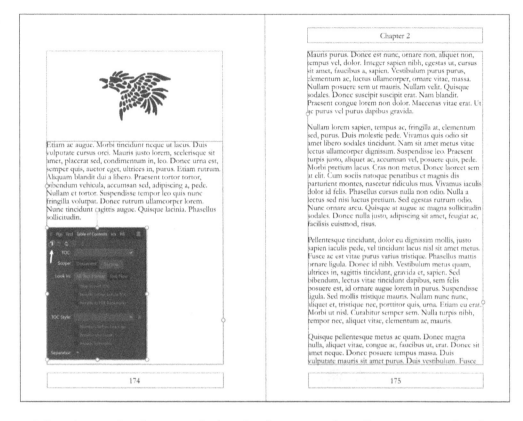

Great. That image is always going to be between that first paragraph of text and that second paragraph of text. We like that.

But the reason I don't use it is because I don't like that appearance there. I want the image centered. And I personally struggle to get an image like that centered on the page.

You can open the Pinning panel (which we'll do in a moment) and go to the Inline tab and then change the Borders values to move the image from the left-hand edge of the text frame. It just never works well for me. It requires too much manual effort.

It's possible there is a way to do that easily, I've just never mastered it. The other issue I have with just directly inserting images is when I need a border around them. You can add a border to an inserted image using the Stroke option in the dynamic menu up top. Click on the white rectangle with a line through it and choose a line color and width.

But the challenge I've run into here in the past is that you had to do it for every single image separately. I just tested it and the good news is that the new Style Picker Tool will work to transfer a border from one image to another.

We covered that briefly in Part 1, but as a reminder, go to the Color Picker Tool towards the bottom of the list of tool options and click on the white arrow to expand the list to see the Style Picker Tool. Click on it. Click on the image with the border you want to copy, and then click on the image that you want to apply that border to, and the Style Picker Tool will also put a border around that second image.

So that makes using inline images less of a problem than it used to be for me before, but I still don't like trying to get an image placed on the page. This could be a me issue, not a them issue, so feel free to experiment.

The other option for placing an image that I also don't use is to pin the image. You can click on an image you've already placed and use the Float with Text option from the top menu or click on Float in the Pinning panel.

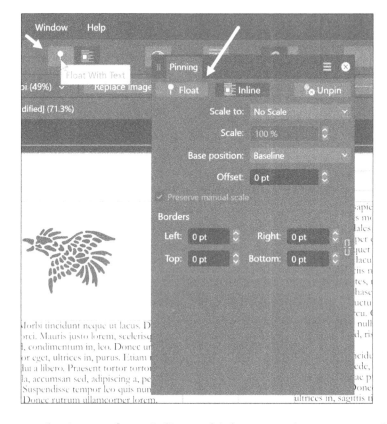

Both will convert the image from inline, which means it gets treated like a line of text, to pinned, which means it will still move with the text, but is not treated like a line of text. It sort of floats around near the text and you can move the "pin" that anchors the image to that text.

Here I've converted the second inserted image to Float and you can see that I was then able to click on it and drag it around but that there is a little blue pin with a line that connects that image to that point.

In the Pinning panel there are options for horizontal alignment of the image. Here I've used Inside Center of the text with an offset of 0 to place the image and it looks decent, but that took three adjustments to get that look:

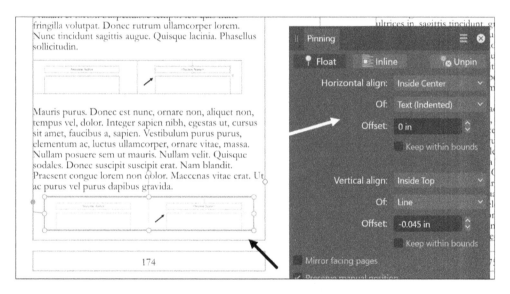

Also, when I change the master page that applies here back to Text and Text, so move the text upward on the page, the image does move with the text, but see how it overlaps the text that comes after it:

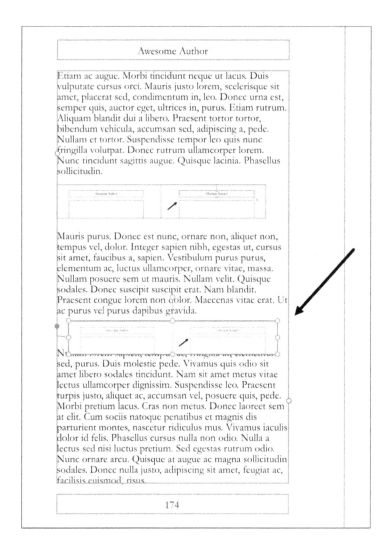

I could go in and adjust the Show Text Wrap Settings on that image to make the text jump the image to get rid of that overlap and then try to reposition it, but for me personally it's just a lot of effort involved when I have a better solution, which is using picture frames.

Now, to be clear, my method has flaws, too. If you add a bunch of text to your document, images in picture frames do not move, so you will have to manually reposition those images. But since I try to do all of my editing outside of Affinity, when I come to Affinity my text is final or almost final, so I can place my images without worrying that later edits will mean I have to reposition them.

Let me show you.

First off, as I write a document, I leave a note that the document needs an image at a specific point. Which means that when I drop my text into Affinity it looks something like this:

During the stage of book formatting when I'm walking through the document from start to finish and applying my master pages for chapter starts and looking for widows/orphans/short lines etc. that need fixing, I also insert my images.

The goal is to have every page final by the time I move on to the next.

Here I'd see that I need to insert an image and I would click on the Picture Frame Rectangle Tool:

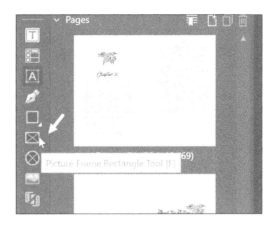

Next, I would left-click and drag onto the document at about the point where it says I need an image until I have a rectangle showing on top of my text. Like this:

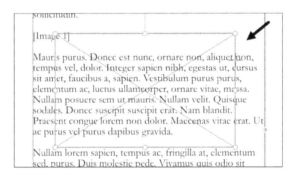

After the picture frame has been inserted into the document, I go to the Show Text Wrap Settings option up top and click on it to open the Text Wrap dialogue box. I then click on the Jump option:

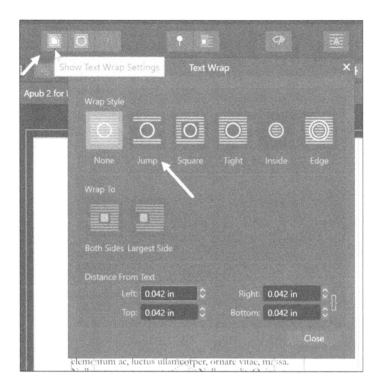

This should move the text that was under that picture frame rectangle to below the rectangle:

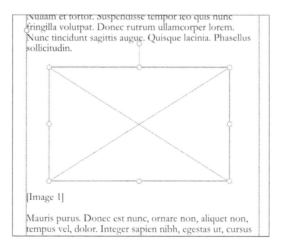

Now I can click on the Place Image Tool and find the image I want to bring in.

The image is going to come into the picture frame in various ways depending on your picture frame settings which can be found under Properties when you're clicked onto the picture frame:

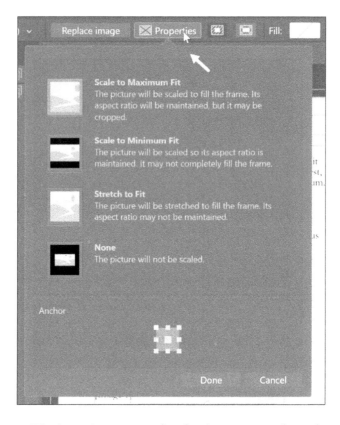

Scale to Maximum Fit is going to scale the image so that the picture frame is filled on either the horizontal or vertical axis, whichever makes more sense given the image shape compared to the picture frame shape. This means you may have part of the image out of frame.

Scale to Minimum Fit will scale the image so that it fits within the picture frame and is completely visible within the frame. But that means you will have space around the image if the image and the frame are not the exact same dimensions.

Stretch to Fit will stretch the image so that it fits within the picture frame. This will distort the image along one axis unless the frame and the image have the exact same proportions.

None just brings the image in at the document DPI, which in our case is 300. If you're going to use None, change that Properties setting before you bring the image in.

Here are all four used on the same image, I've added a border to the picture frames just so you can see them:

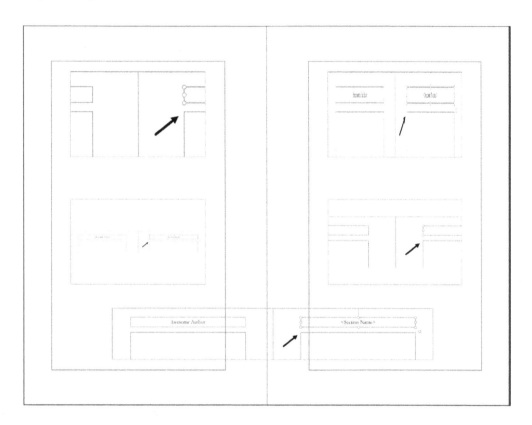

Top left is scaled to maximum fit. Below that is scaled to minimum fit. The top right is stretched to fit (and you can see the skew in the text that results). Below that is the None with our default DPI of 300. And across the bottom is how the image looks just dropped onto the page without using a picture frame.

For a document like we're creating here, I want to use None as my setting. That brings the image in at the largest possible size for the specified DPI, and I know that I can either use the image as-is or make it smaller from there.

Next step is to adjust the picture frame to the image. You can do that by clicking on Size Frame to Content in the dynamic menu up top:

From there you can adjust the frame and image size together using the blue circle located outside the perimeter of the frame in the bottom right corner. Just left-click on that circle and drag at an angle:

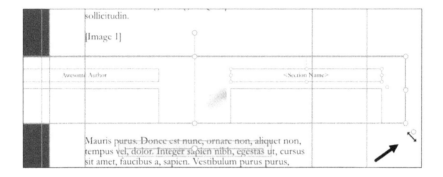

That should resize the frame and the image together.

You can use the slider underneath the frame to change just the image size, but if you do that it won't change the frame size and you'll have to click on Size Frame to Content once more to change the frame to fit the image.

(Or you could resize the image first and then size the frame to the content, but with a picture frame you're only going to see the part of the image that falls within the borders of the picture frame.)

You can also use the Transform panel to resize your image, just make sure to Lock Aspect Ratio when you do so to keep the image proportionate. (If you ever do stretch an image out of proportion Affinity will let you know that has happened in the Preflight panel.)

We want the frame and the image to be the same size because our next step, if it isn't already like this from using it before, is to add a border to the picture frame.

To do that, click on the frame and then click on the white rectangle next to Stroke in the dynamic menu up top. Next, go to the Swatches tab and click on the black swatch:

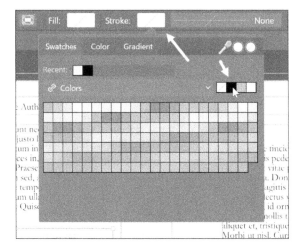

If the line isn't wide enough to be visible, you can adjust it by clicking on that white line to the right of the Stroke rectangle. That will open a dialogue box where you can then use a slider to adjust the line width or you can input a value for line width.

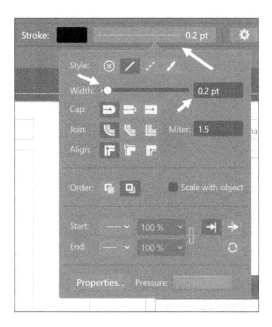

The nice thing about using a picture frame for this is that the next time you insert a picture frame in the document it will default to already having the same border that you used the last time and it will also default to the None import setting.

Which means that for all other images you insert into your document you just have to tell Affinity to jump the frame and then position it.

To position your image, click on the Move Tool and then left-click onto the picture frame and drag the image into position. You can also left-click onto the image and use the arrow keys to fine-tune your positioning.

I use the Snapping lines to make sure the image is centered in the middle of the text frame. Affinity will show center lines for both the overall page as well as just the text frame, so be sure you choose the center line for the text frame and not the overall page since the margins on book pages are uneven.

I usually do this visually, but if you bring the image in from the outer edge of the page, the first center line you encounter will be the correct one.

If you have multiple images on a page, sometimes it helps to hide the other images while centering an image. To do that, click on the little gray circle for that image layer in the Layers panel. It will turn a darker gray color when the layer is hidden as you can see here:

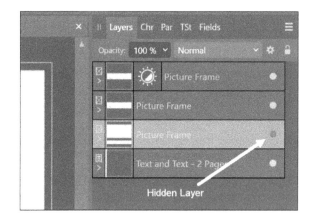

Just be sure to unhide the image again afterward by clicking on that circle once more.

Once an image is centered left to right, you can also move it up and a down a bit using the arrow keys to see where it's best to place it between the lines of text. I usually find that there is a spot that results in equal distance between the line above and the line below.

Also, sometimes you can "push" the text below the image down one line or "raise" it one line by moving the image slightly, but you can only move an image so far before more text jumps the image, so watch out for that. The line that is meant to be below the image will suddenly be above it or vice versa.

Note that this will work somewhat differently if you choose to wrap text around the picture frame rather than jump it.

Finally, my last step is to delete that text that says [Image 1] because I no longer need it to tell me to insert that image. I also often will format the paragraph below an image to remove the indent from that paragraph, but that's a matter of personal preference.

Note that when I'm doing this I am moving back and forth between using various tools. So when I'm moving a picture frame around I have the Move Tool selected but when I delete the text that said [Image 1] I have to click on the Artistic Text Tool before doing that. So if something isn't working for you, check that you have the right tool selected.

Now, one other issue to address here when using picture frames to put images into your document is that the picture frame will stay where you put it. The frame is not tied to your text. If you insert text in your chapter and that moves the rest of the text down, you'll need to also manually move any picture frames past that point to account for that.

But more commonly the issue is that the text does not naturally fall in a way that works with the picture frame.

Let's look at an example here of what I mean. I need to insert another image here where it says Image 2:

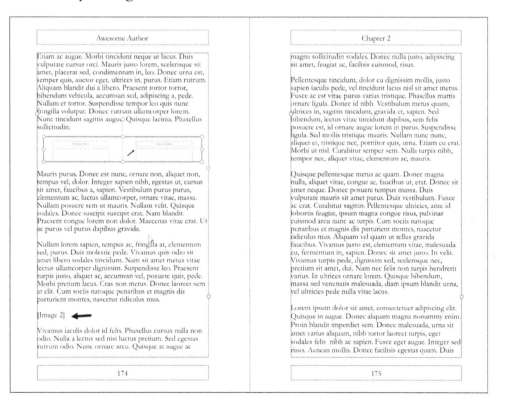

But the image I need to insert is too big for the space that's left at the bottom of the page. Here I've brought it in at the top of the next page where it can actually fit:

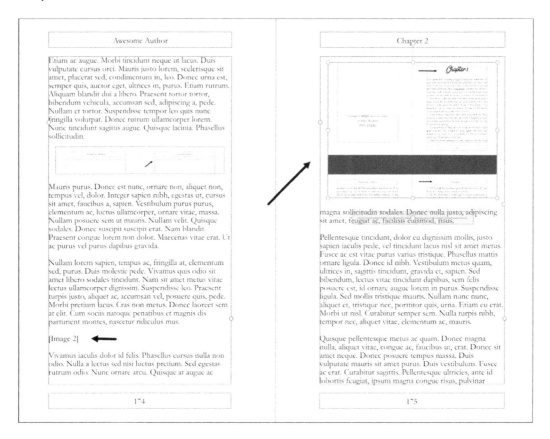

The problem is, the text is still on the other page, because of the way the text naturally flows across the text frames. To fix this, I have to manually add a frame break to push the text from [Image 2] onward to the next page.

I covered that in the last book, but as a reminder, click where you want the break, and go to Text→Insert→Breaks→Frame Break.

This will push all of that text forward to the next text frame. Delete the placeholder text and you end up with something like this:

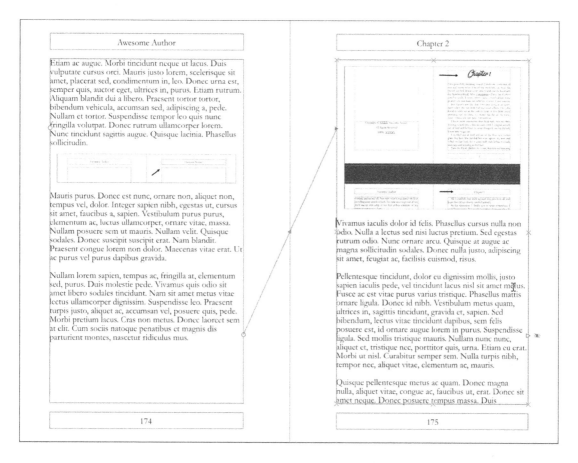

You could also explore other options in a scenario like this. I will sometimes see if I can move an explanatory paragraph above the image instead of having it below the image, for example, if the gap is really big. Or I may make other images a little smaller earlier in the chapter if that helps me bring an image to the bottom of the prior page. Or, if there's room to do so, I might increase the size of an image a bit to push text down.

But sometimes (as you've seen if you have the print version of this book) I just leave that white space there.

Another option that I don't use is to change the text wrap setting. I always jump the image, but you could have the text wrap around the side of the image instead, especially for any image that only takes up a small part of the page.

Like here where I've set the text to wrap around the larger side of an image and moved the image to the left-hand side of the text frame:

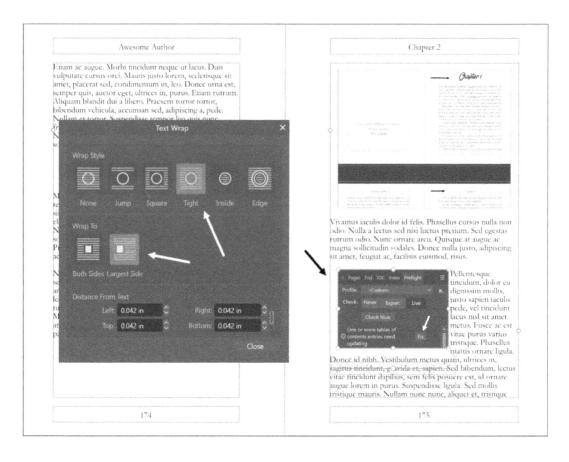

* * *

One final note that I'm adding to the end of this chapter: When I was formatting the first book in this series in Affinity I noticed that sometimes my picture frame setting would reset from None to Scale to Maximum Fit and the next image I imported into the picture frame was the wrong dimensions. To fix this I'd Undo and then change the Properties setting back to None.

I suspect the reason this happened a handful of times was because I accidentally clicked on the Clear Fill on Populate option which is in the dynamic menu right next to the Size Frame to Content option. So I'm adding a caution here to be sure you don't click the wrong option. And, if you do, to let you know you just need to go and change that Properties setting back to None once more.

Also, I wanted to more specifically mention here that when you're working with a picture frame and add an image to that frame that the image will be its own layer underneath that frame. If you go to the Layers panel and expand the picture frame layer you'll see a listing for the image underneath. You can click on that image layer to adjust just the image, but will then need to adjust the frame as well after the fact. I try to stay at the picture frame layer level as much as possible because that should adjust them both, but there have been times I needed to drop down to the image layer instead, so I wanted to let you know that's possible.

This is especially likely to be needed if you change the picture frame dimensions using the Transform panel, because the dimensions of the underlying image may not change to match.

Okay, so that was placing images in your document, now let's talk about adjusting them.

IMAGE ADJUSTMENTS

This may be something I am doing wrong, but I found with my setup using the greyscale 8 setting in Affinity (as recommended by IngramSpark) and then generating as a PDF and sending off to Amazon KDP or IngramSpark, that my images needed to be manually adjusted to print well.

Images that are mostly white with black lines I have to darken and images that are mostly black I have to lighten.

You may have a different experience. I would recommend ordering a proof copy the first time you generate a book in black and white that has a lot of images using Affinity to see what your specific outcome is.

I am by no means an expert on image adjustment. I think there are people out there who manually adjust every single image in a book with detail and care. Me, I say, "that's a lighter image, let's darken it up some" and "that's a darker image, let's lighten it up some."

What you decide to do will be up to you, but let me see if I can't demonstrate this for you.

Below is a darker image from earlier in the book, unadjusted first and then adjusted:

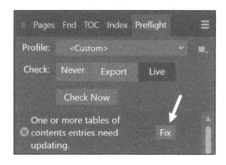

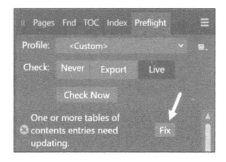

For the ebook you are seeing a screenshot of this. You can see that the lower image is more gray than black and I personally think the text is a little bit more visible.

Here is the same thing for a lighter-colored image that I've darkened:

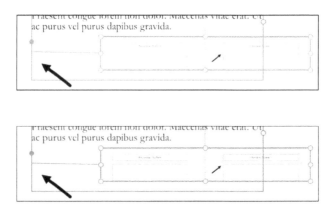

In this case I think the lines come out darker in the second image than the first which makes them a little easier to see.

This is a matter of personal preference. You may disagree with the adjustments or think I didn't take them far enough. Or think there's a better way to adjust them.

But let me show you what I'm doing here. Go to the Layers panel and click on the layer for the image you want to adjust.

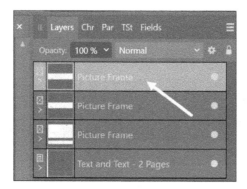

At the very bottom of the Layers panel, you will see a trio of icons:

The one I use is for Adjustments. Click on that to see a dropdown menu (that drops upward) that lists a large number of potential adjustments you can apply. The one I use is Brightness and Contrast. Clicking on that opens a Brightness/Contrast dialogue box:

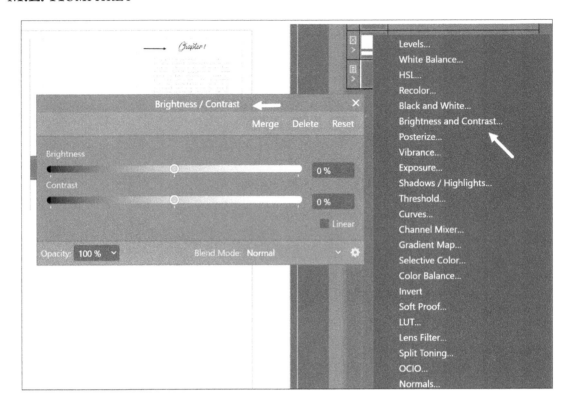

I then either change the brightness value to 35% for dark images or -25% for light images.

Again, I will remind you that I probably do not do this in an ideal way. But if you're reading this in print and could read the images to this point, it worked well enough.

Once you've added an adjustment to a layer, it will show as part of that layer in the Layers panel:

If you click on the little arrow on the left-hand side of the layer to expand it, you can then click on the icon for the adjustment to open that dialogue box once more.

You can also right-click on the adjustment layer and delete it. Or if you want to keep the adjustment but remove it for now, click on the gray circle at the end of the layer row to hide the adjustment.

There is another way to reach the adjustment options and that is through the menu up top. Click on your layer and then go to Layer→New Adjustment→Brightness/Contrast from there.

As you can see in that dropdown menu there are a lot of other image adjustment options available.

There is also a Layer Effects dialogue box. You can open it by using the right-most of those three icons at the bottom of the Layers panel or by going to Layer→Layer Effects.

The Layer Effects dialogue box lets you add shadows, glow, color overlays, etc. I find I use the Layer Effects for cover design or ad images, but not for simple images in book layouts. I'm just mentioning it here so that you know about it.

So, to summarize images. You have three options for placing images in the main body of your document. I prefer to use picture frames. If you use those, insert the picture frame, change the settings so that your text jumps the frame, bring in the image using the None setting, resize as needed and fit the frame to the picture, place the image using your Snapping lines, and then adjust the brightness of the image as desired.

Okay. On to the messiest topic, combining files to create a collection or omnibus.

MERGE MULTIPLE BOOKS

The way I typically will build a book that contains more than one book is to start with the first book in the collection. So let's do that.

I created these books in the original version of Affinity, so it gives me a warning message when I try to open the file:

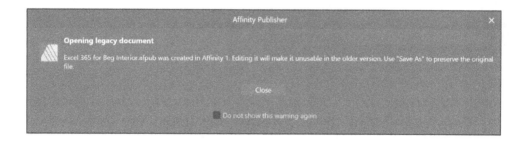

Make sure you have a copy of the original saved somewhere just in case if that happens to you.

Okay. First step is to insert a new title page after the first two page spreads. (Depending on the front matter of your book, you may want to insert the new title page somewhere else. For me, I like to put it after the also by listing but before the table of contents.)

I right-click on pages 2 and 3 of the document and choose Add Pages.

I want 2 pages, After, page 3, using the Title Page master page.

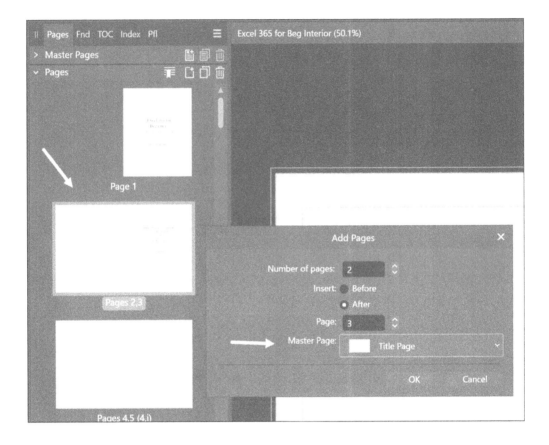

Now select the Artistic Text Tool and go to the first page, the original title page of the document, and copy the text in that text frame. Go back to the newly-inserted title page and paste that text into the text frame there.

Once that's done, you can go back to page 1 and change the title information there to the name of the collection.

(I find it easier to do it this way rather than insert a new Title Page at the beginning of the document because that first page being just a right-hand page has given me interesting results in the past when I tried to insert pages before it.)

Next step is to review the copyright notice and also by pages. For me, I need to update my copyright notice with the new ISBN and year.

After that, we need to insert a new table of contents page spread for the entire collection. I want to place that table of contents in front of the new title page for the first book but after my also by page, and I'm going to leave that blank for the moment.

Here we are. This is our new front matter:

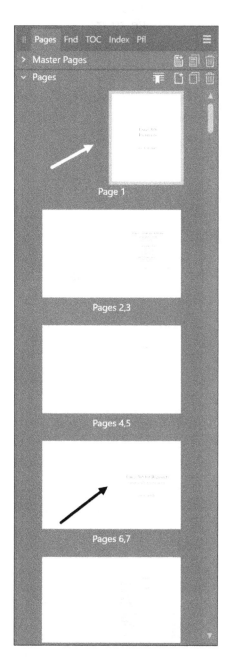

You can see the first page is the title page for the collection, followed by a copyright and also by page spread, followed by a table of contents for the collection, followed by a title page spread for the first book, and then the table of contents for the first book.

That's the easy part. Now we have to go to the end of this book and delete out any back matter that more appropriately belongs at the end of the collection. And we need to leave a left-hand page for the last page spread so that the next book comes in appropriately, because Affinity treats the first page spread in each book as just a single-page spread. So if you don't have a page to push that first page to start on the right the whole next book will be on the wrong side of the page.

Here is the back matter I need to delete:

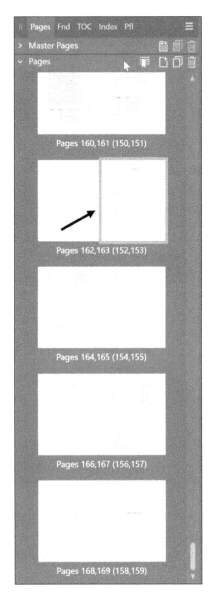

Pages 153 through 159 which include my Index and my About the Author.

After you delete pages from the back of your document, check that you have no text overflow markers in your main text. On occasion I will have my text flow through to my about the author section. When I do that it becomes a problem if I then delete the about the author page, because the text is still there. Just because I took the page where you could see the text away that did not erase that text.

This is why I usually try to keep my about the author page and any back matter separate from the main body of my book. But I am not perfect and sometimes I mess that up. So check for the little red marks along the perimeter of your text frames in the main body of your book to see if this is an issue you need to fix.

If it is, I find the easiest way to fix it is to Undo and bring back the pages I just deleted, delete that text from the about the author page, and then delete the pages again.

You can also just click into the last text frame now available and start deleting text until there's no longer an indication of hidden text that's overflowing the frame. But that's harder because you're working blind and don't know how much to delete. Okay.

So delete the pages that are back matter. Also delete any note that might be at the end of this book telling readers the next book to read. (Something I do in my fiction titles.)

At that point, you should have something that looks like this:

Note the blank left-hand page at the end.

Right-click on that page and choose Add Pages from File from the dropdown menu.

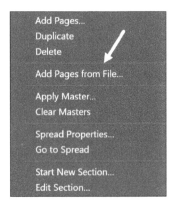

This will bring up an Open dialogue box. Find the next file you want to bring in and click on Open.

That will bring up the Add Pages dialogue box:

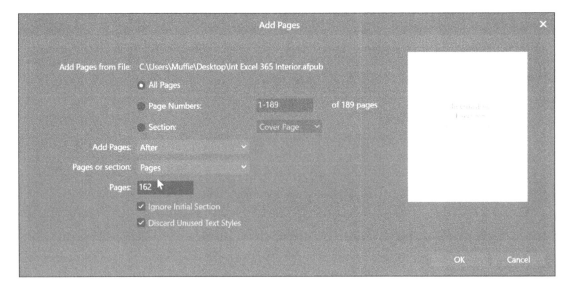

I choose to bring in All Pages, After the last page of my section. There is a checkbox there where Affinity can be told to Ignore Initial Section if you don't want your front matter, but I choose to bring it in because it has my title page. I also leave Discard Unused Text Styles checked because combining files can get messy when it comes to text styles and the less you have to deal with the better.

So basically I don't change anything here, I just click on OK.

Most likely the next thing you will see is an Imported Text Styles dialogue box which is going to show you text styles that Affinity is bringing in from the new file that aren't in the existing one. It will also indicate when there is a conflict, so two text styles with the same name that don't match exactly:

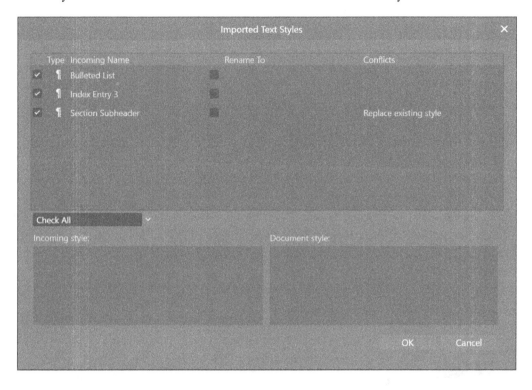

In the dialogue box above you can see that I had a bulleted list text style that is only used in the second book as well as a third-level Index Entry text style only used in the second book. Those are fine and don't require any sort of decision.

But the third line is telling me that I used different formatting for my section subheader between the two books. I don't want to have one overwrite the other because it could impact my text placement which is going to impact my page breaks and images, potentially.

So I click on the Rename To box and Affinity assigns that section subheader text style that's being brought in a unique name:

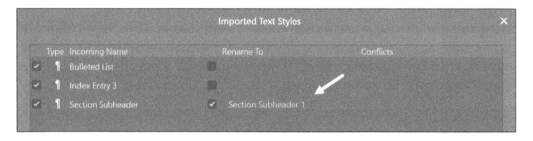

Great. Now I know that both books will be formatted the way they were originally. I can scan through later and see if the difference between the two subheaders is so noticeable it needs to be changed, but in this case it's likely not going to be a problem.

The folks at Affinity envision this merging different files option as something to use for group collaboration. In that case, where it's different sections of one book being brought together, you probably would want to overwrite one or the other text style rather than keep both.

Okay. Done.

Affinity brings in my entire second book and because I had that single blank left-hand page at the end, the title page, etc. are all where they should be:

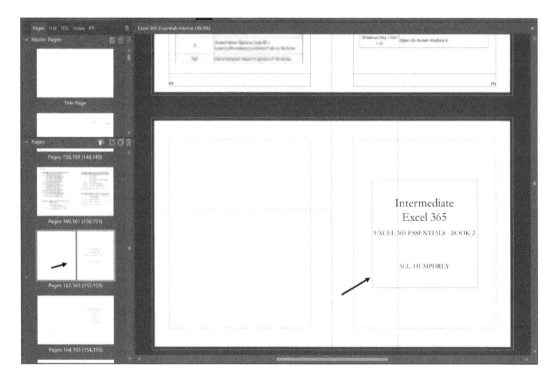

For this one, I need to delete the individual book copyright notice. (I used to leave them in but Amazon made me remove them at some point so now I just have the collection copyright page but not individual pages for the individual books.) I also don't need the also by information, so that entire spread can go.

That leaves me the title page for book two, the table of contents for book two, and then the rest of book two.

At the moment the page numbering is going to be off, because this book is set to restart page numbering at the first chapter. I'm going to fix this later. But keep in mind it's an issue.

I now get to rinse and repeat for as many additional books as I want to add to this collection, omnibus, what-have-you until I've added all of the books I want to include.

I only had one more to add, so I dropped it in, deleted the copyright and also by pages, and that was it. I leave the backmatter of the last book in place.

But what if you didn't have a book that conveniently ended with a left-hand page? How do you get one single page when you've been using two-page master pages?

What I do is insert a new page spread at the end that includes a blank left-hand page. So a No Text and whatever master page:

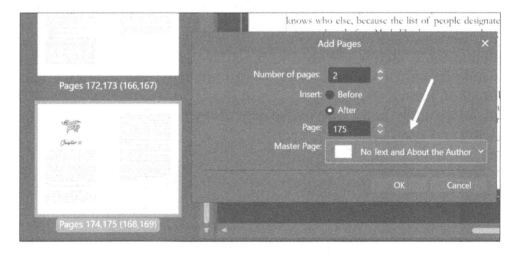

Next, I select just the right-hand page and right-click and choose to Delete it.

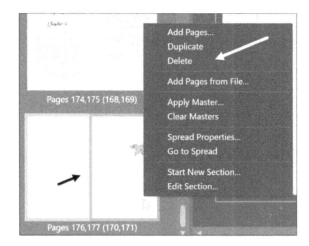

Note how the blue border showing which pages are selected is only around the right-hand page.

Okay, back to this other book we were formatting. Now that I have all my content in one book it's time to make it all work together.

The first thing to consider is how you had structured your chapter headers. I'm in luck with this one because it's a non-fiction title, which means I already had my headers formatted to use the chapter name. That means I don't have to make any adjustment there.

If you were instead using the book title, which you probably would do for most fiction titles, then you'll need to update your master pages to use section names and create sections for each book you imported and assign the book title as that section name.

Here, for example, is the Section Manager for a collection of three novels and a short story of mine:

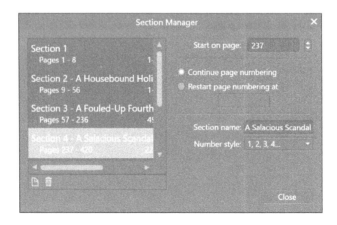

I have the third title selected here. You can see that each story or novel has its own page range assigned and the section name listed is the title of the novel or short story. Also, note that the page numbering is set to continue, not restart.

So do that if you need to do it for your book. Set each section name to match the book in question and while you're there check to continue page numbering through the whole book.

For mine, which is already fine in terms of the header, I need to go to the front matter for each individual title after the first title and make sure that all of those sections continue page numbering.

I right-click on any thumbnail in my book and choose Edit Section to bring up the Section Manager. (That's easier than trying to locate the start of each book in a five-hundred page document.) I can then scroll through the section listing on the left-hand side and look for any numbering listed on the right of that entry that is either in Roman numerals or restarts at 1:

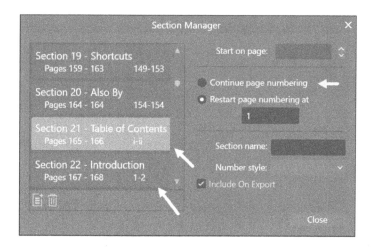

Here you can see the table of contents for the second book I added, for example. Section 21 is the table of contents for that book and currently it's using Roman numerals and also restarted the page numbering. Section 22 is the first chapter of that book which restarted page numbering at 1.

Both of those sections need to be edited to Continue Page Numbering and/or use the 1, 2, 3, 4, etc. numbering style. So I click on each one and make those changes.

Good news is that once I change Section 22 to continue page numbering, the rest of that book's page numbering will be fine because all other sections in the book were already set to continue page numbering.

So it's usually only two sections at most per book that was added that need to be updated. But be sure to scroll through the entire listing of sections to see if that page numbering on the right-hand side is continuous from page 1 of your document to the end.

The next step is for books that use an index. You should have left in the index for the last book you added. Go to the Index panel and look at your entries:

I can tell by the page numbers listed next to the entries in the panel that there are entries listed for all three of my books. The fact that I have some there with page 53 and some with page 367 means that the entire book is covered.

But note that the Index in the document itself is only showing entries right now for the last book. 3D Models, for example, are listed in my Index panel but not my document.

Easy enough to fix, just hit refresh at the top of the Index panel. But note that because you're combining multiple books that may push your index past the number of pages you had allotted to it for the last book:

Index

3D Models 197	Bold Text 100
A	Borders Around Cells 100–104
ABS 512	All Borders 106
Addition 88, 359	Clear 107
Align Text 97–98	Draw Border 105
Analysis ToolPak, Enable 331	Draw Border Grid 102–103, 105
AND 491–493, 512	Format Cells dialogue box 106–107
Angle Text 98–99	
Arrow keys 45	Line Color 105, 107
Arrow, Definition 23, 163	Line Style 104, 107
Auto-Suggested Text 56–57	Slanted line 107
Autocorrect Options, Edit 330	Budget Worksheet 3
AutoSave Settings, Edit 330	**C**
AutoSum 386–387	Cell Notation 83, 164, 345–346
AVERAGE 395–397, 402, 479	Columns 84
AVERAGEA 395–397, 490	Multiple Cells 83
AVERAGEIF 452, 454	Rows 84
AVERAGEIFS 451–454, 457–458	Workbooks 84
B	Worksheets 84

521

See the red circles along the perimeter of the text frame there. These indicate that I have more index entries than text frames for them to flow to.

Which means I need to insert a new page spread (or more than one) for index entries and then flow the existing entries to them.

In this case, I had to add ten more pages to the index. I could have deleted my Also By and auto-flowed my text and Affinity would have done it for me, but I did it manually and flowed the text manually as well.

If you have an index, you should also read through it at the end and make sure that you have no situations where you used Definition, Select in one book but Select, Definition in another or anything similar where the entries need to be combined and streamlined.

If so, make those updates in the Index panel just like you would with a singular book.

Also, this is another reminder of why making custom edits to an index should be avoided as much as possible. Because any edits like that you did in the individual books were lost when you refreshed this index.

Okay, next up, tables of contents.

With novels that don't have named chapters, you're probably in luck because the only table of contents you need is at the front and is the title of each book. If you have a title page that lists the title, that's going to be very easy to create, you just need to know the Text Style that was used for that. In my case that text style is Book Title.

But if you used a cover image for your title page, that may be trickier. In that case, I'd recommend creating a text frame on that title page, typing your title into the frame, and assigning a text style to that title that you can use to feed a table of contents. You can then either hide that layer by clicking on the gray circle in the Layers panel or you can left-click and drag on that layer in the Layers panel to place it below the layer that contains the cover image.

Basically, create a layer on that page that has your title so Affinity can use it to create the table of contents, but then hide it somehow so it doesn't print on that page.

I do not recommend manually creating a table of contents.

Okay, so let's go build my main table of contents for this non-fiction book because there's one more trick I need to show you.

I want to go to page 5 of my overall document, click into the text frame, open the Table of Contents panel, and click on the Insert option.

Once Affinity has inserted a "no table of contents entries found" message on the page, I can then click on Book Title to bring in the title of my three books into my table of contents.

I have one issue, though, which is the Index and About the Author don't use that format. They both use the Chapter Title format. If I want to include them in my table of contents at the beginning (and also not have them listed in the table of contents for the last book), I need to assign them a new text style.

It can be identical to the chapter title style. It just needs to have a different name.

So I go to the first page of the Index, click on the header text at the top of the frame (Index), go up to the dropdown for the text style, and choose to create a new style. I'm going to call that new text style Backmatter.

Once I've created that new text style, I can then go to my About the Author page, click onto that text at the top of the frame, and assign the Backmatter text style to that one as well.

As far as a reader is concerned, my Index and About the Author text will match my chapter header text. But as far as Affinity is concerned, they use different text styles, so I can have a table of contents pull in those two entries without pulling in all of my chapter titles, too.

Now I can go back to that first table of contents and check the box to include any entries that use the Backmatter text style in the table of contents.

Because this is a new table of contents I also need to change the formatting for the entries in the table of contents to use Garamond and small caps. Small caps can be applied through the Typography section of the Character panel as can all caps.

Be sure to update those text styles as soon as you make that change.

I also need to tell Affinity to show page numbers: (If you update your text formatting in your table of contents but don't update the text style and then click on the option to show page numbers, Affinity will revert to the original text style.)

If you use more than one text style to populate your table of contents, like I have here, both will need to be formatted and updated separately.

And here we are:

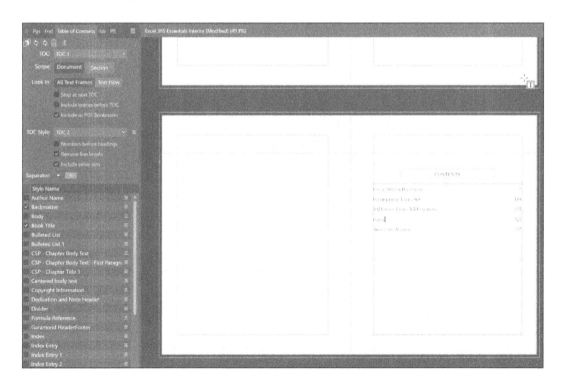

If you look on the left-hand side you can see that this is TOC 1, it does not stop at the next TOC, and it uses Backmatter and Book Title for the text styles that feed the table. Also, in the main document you can see that I've formatted the text and included page numbers.

That was the easy one.

Now we need to go to the next table of contents, which for me is on page 9 of my document. I should be able to click onto that table of contents and my Table of Contents panel should switch over to reflect that I'm now editing TOC 2. But I have had it in the past not be so reliable. So always check that TOC dropdown at the top of the Table of Contents panel before you start making changes.

This table of contents needs to be set so that it stops at the next TOC or else it will list all chapters in the entire document, which we don't want. (The other way to get around that would be if each document had different text styles assigned to those chapters, but I don't do that.)

The Style Name should already be set to the correct text style from when you imported it.

If the table doesn't update automatically, then you will want to update it manually. Now, one thing to keep in mind when updating a table of contents is that you have two options available:

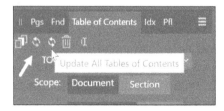

The first one, if you hold your mouse over it, just says Update. The second one says Update All Tables Of Contents. Be careful when you have multiple tables of contents to use the Update option not the Update All. (No matter which option you use, you'll want to go back through the document at the very end and check all of your tables of contents anyways, but if you get one working it is best to leave it alone.)

Okay, so I did that. The next step is to scan the entries and see if there's anything there that shouldn't be or any formatting that needs to be fixed, etc.

Good news is I have formatted table of content entries, they stop at the end of this particular title, and the chapter names look like what they should.

But, I have an issue:

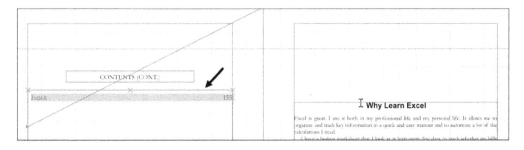

It's showing an entry for index and it shouldn't be.

We deleted the index from this one. We changed the index text style at the end of the entire book. And we're stopping at the next table of contents. So somewhere in my first document here, there is hidden text for index that is formatted as a chapter title and I need to track it down and delete it and then update this table of contents.

Also, as soon as I fix that issue I will need to change the master page spread here to a No Text and Chapter Start master page since my table of contents will fit on just one page.

The best way to find a hidden entry is to use the Find and Replace panel. When I did that, it took me to the top of the title page for the second book I added:

Sometimes weird things will happen with text in Affinity and instead of flowing to the next main body text frame it will flow to a header or footer text frame. It doesn't happen often and usually when it does I can undo and reverse it. But on this one I didn't notice, so now I have to try to fix it some other way.

I cheated to fix it, but it wasn't the ideal solution because that weird text is still hanging out in my document. But since the text was hidden I just selected that search result and changed the assigned text style to none. That meant it was no longer pulled into my table of contents.

Another solution that worked was to reapply the Title master page to that page spread because it should've never had a header so something was wrong there anyway.

Both approaches worked. I updated my table of contents, changed that master page spread, and was ready to move on to table of contents number three.

Okay. Let's do the next table of contents. You can see here that the page numbering needs to update since it currently shows page 1 for the first chapter:

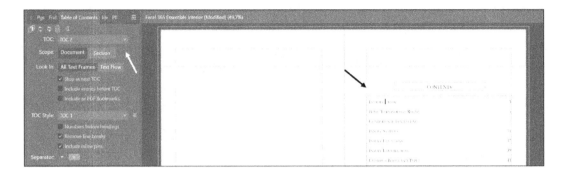

This time when I clicked onto what should be the third table of contents the TOC dropdown menu continued to show TOC 2. I had to manually change the dropdown to TOC 3. So always know which table of contents you're working on in your document and make sure the listed table of contents in the Table of Contents panel matches.

Once I did that and checked the box for "stop at next TOC" it updated just fine, which meant I could move on to the fourth and final one.

That one I also had to change the dropdown in the Table of Contents panel and then it updated fine.

But this was one that I had manually fixed something in for the first book and that issue came back:

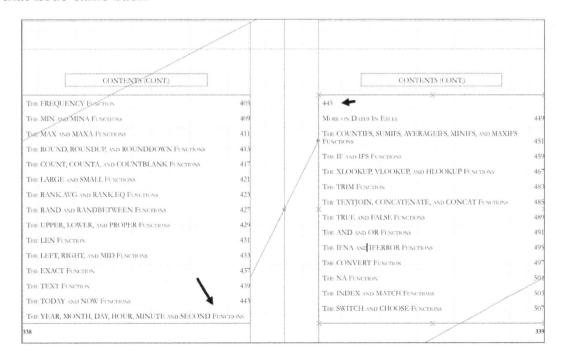

When your chapter names are really long, which mine sometimes are, that is going to impact your table of contents. As you can see here, it pushed the page number to the next line for this chapter. Also, since the page number was now on its own line it is on the left-hand side of the page.

If I click into that line and just type a handful of spaces, that pushes the page number to the right. But I still have the issue that the chapter name is on one page and the page number for that chapter is on the next.

Usually I'd try to fix the chapter name if it was me just being a little too verbose, but in this case that doesn't work. So I'm going to have to manually fix this by clicking into the table of contents and adding an enter to push the chapter listing to the next page:

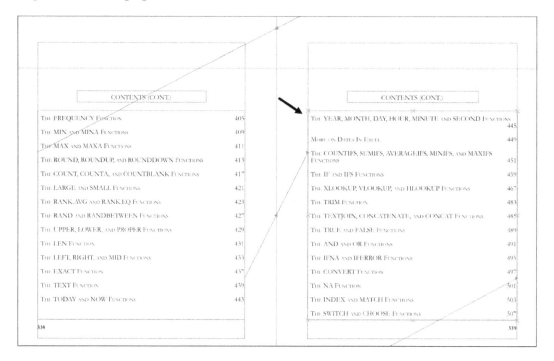

That works fine, but the problem is if I update that table of contents or accidentally choose to update all table of contents, I lose that change. So that edit is probably the absolute last thing I want to do in this document and I need to remember to ignore the Preflight warning that will suggest that I update my table of contents.

At this point we're pretty much done with merging these documents. The next step is to export as a PDF and then page through the entire merged document and look for any issues.

The main issues to check for are that the page numbering continues from the beginning chapter of the first book through to the last page continuous and uses the 1, 2, 3, 4, etc. style. That only necessary front and back matter pages are included. That the back matter is applicable for all of the books and has been updated accordingly. That each book starts on the correct page. That images, if used, are included and in the right location. That all headers and footers are accurate. That any master pages that needed updated have been updated. That all tables of contents in the document are updated and accurate. That the index, if one exists, has been updated and has no similar but not identical entries. And that there are no overflowing text frames anywhere.

MISCELLANEOUS

There are a few tips, tricks, etc. that I didn't cover in the earlier chapters that I want to quickly mention here.

TABLE OF CONTENTS SEPARATOR

By default the table of contents is going to list your text entries on the left-hand side and your page numbers on the right-hand side with a tab as the separator and blank space between the two.

But you can change this.

The Separator option in the Table of Contents panel has a dropdown menu that lets you choose a tab, bullet, em dash, en dash, em space, en space, or any combination of the above. You can also manually add text to that field.

Here, for example, is the main table of contents we used above now using a space, an em dash, and another space to separate the titles from the page numbers:

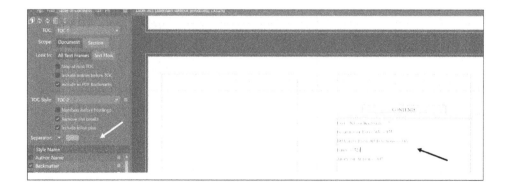

I typed the space, selected the em dash, and then typed the other space into that field, indicated by the arrow in the image above.

Be sure to hit Enter after you choose your separators or it will revert back to the default.

Another one that a lot of people like to use is a dotted line that connects the chapter title and page number. That needs to be applied from the Edit Text Style dialogue box.

Click on the text for one of your chapter listings in the table of contents, go to the Text Styles panel, right-click on the text style being used, and choose Edit [Style Name] from the dropdown menu:

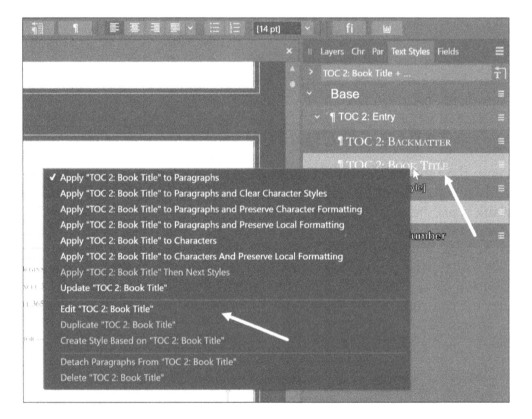

This will bring up the Edit Text Style dialogue box. Go to the Tab Stops option on the left-hand side under Paragraph. If there isn't already a tab stop listed, add one by clicking on the plus sign at the bottom of the black box in the center of the screen:

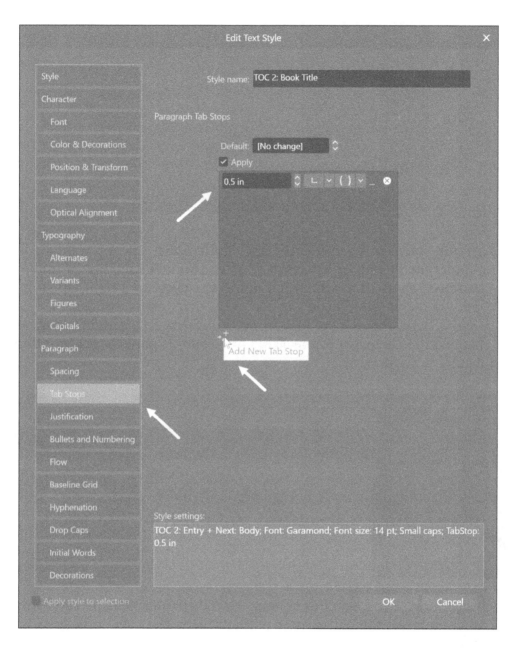

Once you have a tab stop you'll need to change the dropdown for Tab Stop Leader.

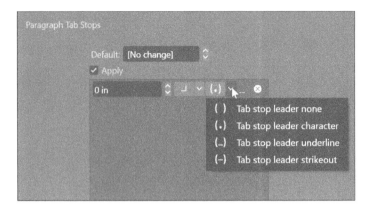

Use Character (.) if you want a dotted line, Underline (_) if you want a solid line that is at underline height, or Strikeout (-) if you want a solid line at midlevel.

You also need to use 0 for the listed numeric value and a right tab stop in the first dropdown menu (which you can see in the screenshot above).

Also, and I think this is new in Affinity Publisher 2.0, it didn't work for me until I changed the Separator in the Table of Contents panel to Right Indent Tab from a regular tab separator:

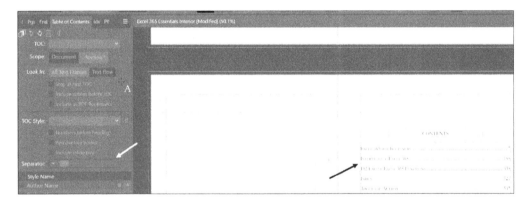

In the image above I've made this change for the chapter titles text style (the first three entries) but not the backmatter text style (the last two entries) so you can see the difference.

EXPORT IMAGE HEAVY BOOKS TO PDF

When I'm just using an accent image in a book in Affinity I export as a PDF/X-1a:2003 file. But for really image-heavy books I use custom settings.

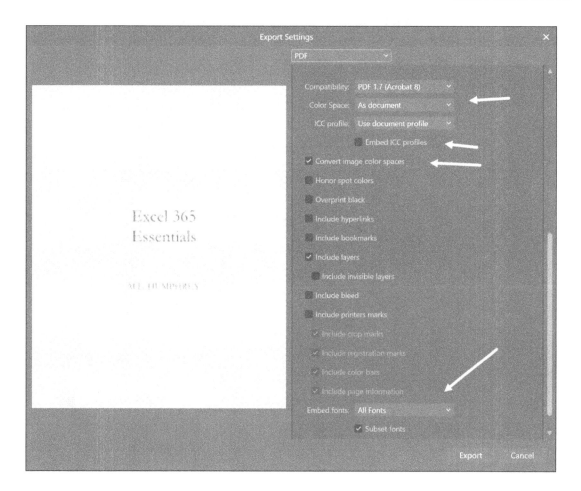

In the Advanced section for Export Settings, I use Compatibility of PDF 1.7, choose a Color Space of "as document", and an ICC profile of "use document profile".

I also make sure that the Embed ICC profiles box is not checked but I do check the Convert Image Color Spaces box. Finally, I make sure that Affinity will include Layers and embed all fonts.

Again, I may not be the expert here, but these settings have worked good enough for me. If you're spending a lot on a print run rather than doing print on demand, work with your printer on exactly what they need. (And if you're really curious, IngramSpark does publish a technical guidelines document that you can try to use as a guide.)

SAVE AN EXPORT PRESET

Because Affinity has the nasty habit (maybe not anymore, but it used to) of defaulting to the last export setting you used, not just for that document but for any Affinity document, I save my black and white export settings as a preset.

To do that, click on the three lines at the top of the Advanced section for a PDF export in the Export Settings dialogue box and choose Create Preset.

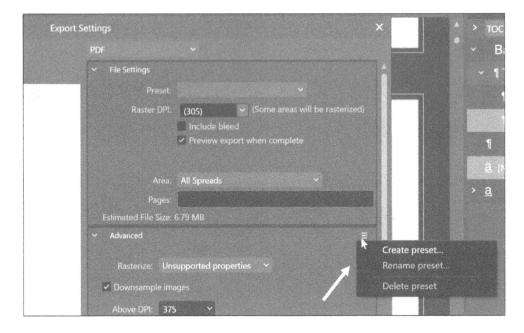

Give the preset a name when the dialogue box appears and click OK. It will then be available in your Preset dropdown menu so that you never have to think about it again.

CREATE A KEYBOARD SHORTCUT

You can create custom keyboard shortcuts in Affinity.

For example, I have a keyboard shortcut that automatically opens the Brightness/Contrast setting so that all I have to do to adjust an image is click on it, use my shortcut, and then input my adjustment value. I also recently added one for frame breaks.

To add a keyboard shortcut, go to Edit→Preferences to open the Preferences dialogue box, and click on Shortcuts.

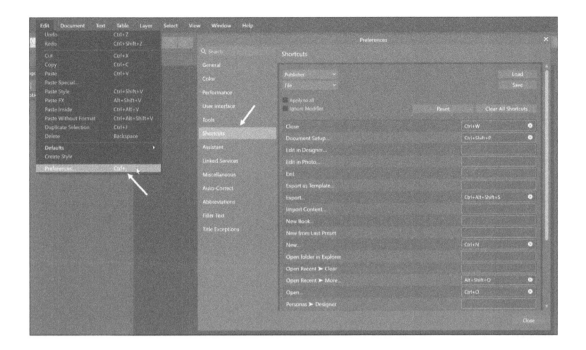

That will show all the available settings or tasks that can be assigned a shortcut. It will also display any shortcut that's already assigned to that setting or task.

You can modify an existing shortcut, although be careful since then your system won't work the way anyone else's does if you do that.

For the one I mentioned above, I used the second dropdown menu up top to choose Layer, and then scrolled down to find New Adjustment →Brightness/ Contrast. I then clicked into the field for that option and typed my shortcut. (I use Ctrl + ~ for that one.)

Click Close when done.

CONCLUSION

Okay, so there you have it, the basics of formatting a print interior using Affinity Publisher 2.0. Part 1 covered a basic title with a simple accent image. Part 2 expanded on that and covered tables of contents, indexes, inserting images into your text, and creating a file that merges multiple books into one.

As I've mentioned elsewhere, this has worked for me for formatting about a hundred books, but I may not have the perfect approach. I am the perennial A-student who does things good enough but not perfect, so if you find a better way to do it or want to do something differently than I showed you here, go for it.

My goal with these books was to short-cut the learning curve for you so that you didn't have to do the same watch videos, experiment, try, try again that I've had to do to learn this program.

Hopefully this helped. If you get stuck, reach out, I'm happy to see if I can find an answer for you.

Also, Affinity has very good help resources, so don't be afraid to do a quick internet search for Affinity Publisher and whatever you're trying to learn. From what I've seen their user forums also tend to be pretty cordial so if you ask a question there someone likely isn't going to jump all over you for not being perfect. (Unlike some other tech forums out there.)

Good luck with it. Don't do it if you hate it. For most books most readers are going to be just fine with a Vellum-formatted or similar book. But have fun with it if you do enjoy it.

The beauty of self-publishing, at least if you're using print on demand, is that you can change things if you want. Try something. Publish it. Decide you don't like it. Change it. Easy peasy.

Okay. Enjoy. And reach out if you get stuck.

APPENDIX A: QUICK TAKES

AUTHOR NAME

FIELD EDIT
Fields panel. Click on field next to Author. Type author name. Enter.

INSERT
Artistic Text Tool. Click on location in document where field should be inserted. Go to Fields panel. Double-click on Author.

BOOK TITLE

FIELD EDIT
Fields panel. Click on field next to Title. Type book title. Enter.

INSERT
Artistic Text Tool. Click on location in document where field should be inserted. Go to Fields panel. Double-click on Title.

CHAPTER TITLE

INSERT AS HEADER
Click on location in document. Go to top menu. Text→Insert Fields→ Section Name. Assign the chapter title to the section.

COLUMNS

BALANCE TEXT
Click on the text frame. Go to the Columns section of the Text Frame panel and click the "Balance Text Columns" box.

CHANGE NUMBER
Move Tool. Click on text frame. Go to dynamic menu up top and change value for Columns. Or use Columns section of the Text Frame panel.

DIVIDING LINE
Click on the text frame. Open the Text Frame panel and go to the Column Rules section and change the Stroke settings. Top and Bottom values will

determine whether the line fills the entire space. Start and End dropdowns can be used to put a shape at the end of the divider line, like an arrow.

FORMAT
Click on the text frame. Open the Text Frame panel and go to the Columns section.

GAP BETWEEN
Click on text frame. Go to dynamic menu up top and change the number in the field to the right of the number of columns setting. Or open the Text Frame panel and go to the Columns section and adjust the value for the gutter.

DOCUMENT PRESET

CREATE
Use the New dialogue box to specify all document settings. When done, click on the icon with a plus sign next to the name for the document. In the Create Preset dialogue box type a name for the document preset, choose an icon, and choose a Category.

DELETE
Right-click on document preset in the New dialogue box and choose Delete Preset.

MOVE DOCUMENT PRESET TO NEW CATEGORY
In the New dialogue box, left-click on the document preset in the document preset listing, and drag to the new category.

NEW CATEGORY
In the New dialogue box, at the bottom of the listing of document presets, click on the icon for Create Category. Type the category name in the New Category dialogue box. OK.

RENAME
Right-click on document preset in the New dialogue box and choose Rename Preset. Type new name into Rename Preset dialogue box. OK.

EXPORT

PDF

To export a PDF of your document, go to File→Export, and choose the PDF option. For review purposes, All Spreads is better because it will keep facing pages together in the PDF. For KDP and IngramSpark upload, use All Pages.

IMAGE

ADJUSTMENTS

To adjust an image, click on the image layer, go to Layer→New Adjustment and choose the type of image adjustment you need. You can also use the Adjustments option at the bottom of the Layers panel.

CENTER

Left-click and drag the image until you see the green center line. For a standard book, be sure to drag from the outer edge of the page because there will be two center lines, one for the entire page and one for the text frame. Lines will only be visible when Snapping is turned on.

For a pinned image, use the Pinning panel.

DPI

The image DPI will increase as your image size decreases. For print, images should have a minimum DPI of 300. You can change the minimum DPI for the document by going to File→Document Setup→Document and changing the DPI setting there.

FLOAT

To float an image, open the Pinning panel and click on the Float tab.

IMPORT PREFERENCES WITH PICTURE FRAME

When importing an image into a picture frame, you can set how the image imports using the Preferences option in the dynamic menu after you click on the picture frame.

INLINE

To make an image an inline image, open the Pinning panel and click on the Inline tab.

INSERT

Place Image Tool. Select image to insert. Open. Image may automatically insert. If not, click and drag in workspace until desired size.

INSERT IN PICTURE FRAME

Click on picture frame layer. Place Image Tool. Select image to insert. Open. Your import preferences will determine if the image comes in at the document DPI or at a size that best fits the picture frame.

MOVE

Move Tool. Click on image layer or directly on image if not in a picture frame. Click on image, hold left-click and drag to desired location. Use Snapping to align along edges or center.

MOVE PIN

For a pinned image, you can left-click and drag on the pin to move what text the image is pinned to.

PIN TO TEXT

If you click into your text before inserting an image, the image will be pinned to your text when it inserts. If an image is not pinned to text, you can use the Pinning panel or the pin option in the dynamic menu up top to pin the image to your text after the fact.

QUALITY

For print files, use a DPI of at least 300 for grayscale images and 600 for black and white line drawings. Go to File→Document Setup to specify your document DPI. Set it slightly above the desired DPI if importing images.

REPLACE

Document top menu. Window→Resource Manager. Select image. Replace. Select new image. Open. Close resource manager.

Or. Move Tool selected, click on image, use Replace Image option in dynamic menu. Choose new image. Open

RESIZE

Move Tool. Click on image layer or directly on image if not in a picture frame.

Option A: Transform panel. Lock Aspect Ratio. Change height or width value.

Option B: Click on blue circle in corner and drag at an angle to resize proportionately. Or click on blue circle along any edge to change height or width only. This will skew most images.

UNPIN

Layers panel. Click on image layer. Open Pinning panel. Click on Unpin.

WRAP

To have text jump or wrap around an inserted image, click on the image and then use the Show Text Wrap Settings in the top menu to choose the Wrap Style.

INDEX

INSERT

Click into document where you want to place the index. Go to the Index panel. Click on the Insert Index option.

Or click into the document, go to the top menu, Text→Index→Insert Index.

MANUAL EDITS

Once inserted, an index can be manually edited but those edits will be overwritten if the index is ever updated.

TEXT STYLE

The index entries use text styles so text can be edited and then the text style updated to apply that change to all entries.

UPDATE

Go to the top menu and then Text→Index→Update Index.

Or use the Index panel and choose the Update option at the top. If the index does not update, delete the existing text of the index, and insert a new index instead.

INDEX MARKERS AND TOPICS

CROSS-REFERENCE
Right-click on the topic you want to cross-reference from and choose Add Cross Reference. In the Add Cross-Reference dialogue box select the topic you want to reference to in the dropdown menu.

INSERT
Select the text you want to use as your index text or click into the text where you want the marker. Either go to the Index panel and click on the Insert Marker option at the top or go to the top menu, Text→Index→Insert Index Mark.

MOVE ENTRY LEVEL
Go to the Index panel and left-click on the topic name you want to move. Drag it to the topic you want to place it under.

Or right-click on the topic name choose to Edit Topic and change the Parent Topic information to either add or remove a parent level.

NAME (ASSIGN)
In the Insert Index Mark dialogue box type the name into the Topic Name field.

NAME (EDIT)
Click once on the name. Click again to select the text. Type in your new name.

Or right-click, Edit Topic, and change the value in the Topic Name field.

PARENT TOPIC (ASSIGN)
Open the Insert Index Mark dialogue box or the Edit Index Mark dialogue box and choose the parent topic you want from the Parent Topic dropdown menu.

PARENT TOPIC (REMOVE PAGE NUMBERING)

To remove any underlying citations from the Parent Topic in the Index panel either move them to a subtopic or delete them by clicking on each entry and using the trash can icon at the top of the panel.

MASTER PAGE

ADD NEW

Pages panel. Master Pages section. Right-click on existing master page.

Option A: Choose Insert Master. Click OK to create a new master page that has the basic properties of the existing master page.

Option B: Choose Duplicate to create an exact duplicate of the existing master page.

MOVE

Pages panel. Master Pages section. Left-click on master page and drag. Blue line along edge will show where master page will move to. Release left-click when positioned where wanted.

RENAME

Pages panel. Master pages section. Click on master page thumbnail. Click on name of master page. Type in new name. Enter.

MERGE DOCUMENTS

ADD DOCUMENT

Go to the page of the existing document in the Pages panel where you want to add the document, right-click, and choose Add Pages From File from the dropdown. Navigate to and select the document to import. In the Add Pages dialogue box choose All Pages, After, Pages, and verify that it shows the page number for that page. OK.

PRE-IMPORT SET-UP

If your documents are set to have a right-hand page start, be sure that the document you're importing into has only one page on the left-hand side at the end in order to maintain pages on the correct side of the page.

PAGE NUMBER

CHANGE NUMBERING STYLE

Pages panel. Pages section. Right-click on page and choose Edit Section. Click on section name that contains the pages where you want to change the numbering style if not already visible. Choose the new style from the Number Style dropdown menu. Close.

INSERT

Master page. Artistic Text Tool. Click where you want page number placed. Go to top menu, Text→Insert→Fields→Page Number.

RESTART AT 1

Pages panel. Pages section. Right-click on page where you want to restart at 1. Start New Section. (Or Edit Section if one has already been started.) Click button for Restart Page Numbering At. Enter 1. Change numbering style if needed. Close.

PAGES

ADD PAGES

Pages panel. Pages section. Right-click on an existing page or page spread. Add Pages. Choose the number of pages to add, whether to insert before or after that location, and choose the master page to use for the inserted pages. OK.

APPLY MASTER PAGE

Pages panel. Pages section. Right-click on the pages where you want to apply the master page. (Be sure that both pages are selected in a two-page spread.) Apply Master. Choose desired master page from dropdown menu. OK.

DELETE PAGES

Pages panel. Pages section. Select pages or page spreads that you want to delete. Right-click. Delete X Pages.

SELECT

If you only want to edit one page in a two-page spread, be sure to click on just that side of the page spread. Only that one page should be surrounded by a blue border.

If there is more than page spread that you want to select, click on the first page or page spread at one end of the page range, hold down the shift key and click on the last page or page spread at the other end of the page range.

PANEL

CLOSE
To close a panel either go to the Window menu and click on the panel name or left-click and drag the panel until it is standalone in your workspace and then click on the X in the top right corner.

MOVE OR ANCHOR
Left-click on panel tab and drag to desired location. To anchor, either drag until you see a blue box appear and then release or drag to where other panels are already anchored and add to those tabs.

OPEN
To open a panel go to the Window menu and click on the panel name. Some panels are listed in secondary dropdown menus.

PICTURE FRAME

BORDER
Click on the Picture Frame. Go to the dynamic menu up top and use the Stroke option to add a color to create a border or click on the line next to it to change the border width.

INSERT
Picture Frame Rectangle Tool. Click and drag to create frame on canvas.

JUMP
To have text jump an inserted picture frame, click on the Picture Frame and then use the Show Text Wrap Settings in the top menu and choose Jump for the Wrap Style.

RESIZE TO IMAGE
Click on Picture Frame and in dynamic menu choose the Size Frame to Content option.

WRAP TEXT AROUND

To have text wrap around an inserted picture frame, click on the Picture Frame and then use the Show Text Wrap Settings in the top menu and choose Square or Tight for the Wrap Style.

RECOVER FILE

RECOVER FILE

If Affinity ever crashes and closes while you were working on a file, reopen the program and try to reopen the file. Affinity should tell you that there is a recovery version of the file available. Choose to open the recovery version and then check for the last edits you made to determine if any of your work was lost and needs to be redone.

SECTION

ASSIGN NAME

Pages panel. Pages section. Right-click on the page at the start of the section and either Edit Section or Start New Section. In Section Manager type name into Section Name field. Close.

CHANGE START PAGE

Pages panel. Pages section. Right-click and Edit Section. In Section Manager, change the "Start On Page".

CONTINUE PAGE NUMBERING

Pages panel. Pages section. Right-click and Edit Section to open Section Manager. Click on the section that needs to continue page numbering and check the box to continue page numbering.

CREATE

Pages panel. Pages section. Right-click on the page that you want to have start the new section, Start New Section. In Section Manager, assign name if desired and verify page numbering format and whether it should restart or continue.

EDIT

Pages panel. Pages section. Right-click and Edit Section.

DELETE

Pages panel. Pages section. Right-click and Edit Section. In Section Manager, click on the section you want to delete and use the small trash can icon to delete it.

INSERT NAME

Click on location in header where field should be inserted. Go to top menu, Text →Insert→Fields→Section Name.

RESTART PAGE NUMBERING

Pages panel. Pages section. Right-click and Edit Section. For the section that needs to restart page numbering, check the box to "restart page numbering at", verify the page number, generally 1, and the number style.

SNAPPING

ENABLE

Go to the horseshoe shaped magnet image in the top center. Click on the dropdown arrow. Check the box next to Enable Snapping.

USE

To use snapping, as you move an object around in your workspace Affinity will show either green or red lines on the workspace when the object is aligned with the edges or center of other objects on the page.

STUDIO PRESET

ADD NEW

Arrange panels as desired. Go to top menu. Window→Studio→Add Preset. Type name. OK.

APPLY

Top menu. Window→Studio. Select desired preset. Or use Ctrl + Shift + [Number] preset for that studio.

DELETE

Window→Studio→Manage Studio Presets. Select preset name. Delete. Close.

RENAME

Window→Studio→Manage Studio Presets. Select preset name. Rename. Type in new name. OK.

SAVE CHANGES

Make desired changes to panel preset arrangement. Window→Studio→Add Preset. Type in exact same name as before. OK. Agree to overwrite old preset.

TABLE OF CONTENTS

ENTRIES (SELECT)

Assign one or more unique text styles to each text entry in the document that you want included in the table of contents. Go to the Table of Contents panel and under Style Name, check the check box for each text style you want to include.

ENTRIES (MANUAL UPDATE)

You can manually update any text in the table of contents, but it is better to update the text in the document and then refresh your table of contents.

ENTRIES (WHEN NO TEXT AVAILABLE FOR SELECTION)

If you ever have a situation where you need a table of contents entry but there is no visible text to use for it, you can create a text frame on that page, place that text you need into the frame, assign a text style to it that you are using in the table of contents, and then hide the frame.

FOR SECTION

To insert a table of contents that covers only a section of a book, insert the table of contents like normal but be sure to check the box for "Stop at Next TOC" and to use different text styles than the ones used in the overarching table of contents.

INSERT

Click into the document where you want your table of contents inserted.

Option A: Go to the Table of Contents panel, click on the Insert option on the left at the top.

Option B: Top menu, Text→Table of Contents→Insert Table of Contents.

OVERARCHING

For a table of contents that covers the entire document when other tables of contents exist in the document, be sure to use specific text styles for just that table of contents and to NOT check the "Stop at Next TOC" option.

PAGE NUMBERS

To include page numbers in your table of contents entries, right-click on the preferences dropdown for that text style and check the box for "Include Page Number." To remove page numbers, uncheck it.

SEPARATORS BETWEEN TEXT AND PAGE NUMBER

Go to the Separator section of the Table of Contents panel. Use the dropdown menu to select your desired separator or type into the field.

For a dotted line or solid line, right-click on the text style in the Text Styles panel, and choose to edit it. Go to the Tab Stops section and choose the desired Tab Stop Leader Character option.

UPDATE

Go to the Table of Contents panel and click on the Update option at the top. If you have multiple tables of contents in your document, be sure the TOC dropdown shows the table of contents you want to update or choose to update all.

Or go to Text→Table of Contents→Update Table of Contents.

Or click on Fix in the Preflight panel when it says one or more table of contents need updated.

TEXT

ADD SPACE BETWEEN LINES

Artistic Text Tool. Select paragraph of text. Paragraph panel. Spacing section. Leading dropdown. Choose desired option. Or for multiple lines of the same style, click on Space Between Same Styles and set a value.

ADD SPECIAL SYMBOLS OR CHARACTERS
Artistic Text Tool. Click into workspace where desired. Go to the Glyph Browser panel. (Window→Text→Glyph Browser if not open.) Find desired symbol or character. Double-click on symbol or character to insert.

ALIGNMENT
Artistic Text Tool. Click on the paragraph or select the paragraphs. Dynamic menu choices above workspace. Four images with lines. Align Left, Align Center, Align Right, or dropdown menu for Justify Left, Justify Center, Justify Right, Justify All, Align Towards Spine, Align Away From Spine. Or, to the right of that, dropdown menu for Top Align, Center Vertically, Bottom Align, Justify Vertically.

The horizontal alignment options are also available at the top of the Paragraph panel.

ALL CAPS OR SMALL CAPS
Artistic Text Tool. Select the text to be formatted. Go to Character panel. Typography section. Click on the two capital Ts to apply all caps. Click on the capital T with a smaller capital T to apply small caps. Check your text entries for issues with using a capital letter or lower case letter when working with small caps because the two do look different in small caps.

BOLD
Artistic Text Tool. Select text. Font Style dropdown menu, Ctrl + B, or click on B in top menu.

Or go to Character panel and choose the Strong option from the Character Style dropdown menu at the top or use the Font Style dropdown menu.

Only works if there is a bold version of the font available.

FONT
Artistic Text Tool. Select text. Top menu, left-hand side. Font Family dropdown. Choose font.

Or select text and go to Character panel and use the Font Family dropdown at top.

HYPHENATION

Artistic Text Tool. Select text. Paragraph panel. Hyphenation section. Click on box next to Use Auto-Hyphenation. Change values as needed.

INDENT PARAGRAPH

Artistic Text Tool. Select paragraph. Paragraph panel. Spacing section. Second option on left-hand side. (First Line Indent). Add value.

ITALICS

Artistic Text Tool. Select text. Font Style dropdown menu, Ctrl + I, or click on I in top menu.

Or go to Character panel and choose the Emphasis option from the Character Style dropdown menu at the top or use the Font Style dropdown.

Only works if there is an italic version of the font available.

JUMP IMAGE

Move Tool. Select image. Click on Show Text Wrap Settings option in top menu. In Text Wrap dialogue box choose Jump as desired Wrap Style.

KEEP TOGETHER

Artistic Text Tool. Select second paragraph that you want to keep together. Go to the Paragraph panel. Flow Options section. Check box for Keep With Previous Paragraph.

LINE SPACING (LEADING)

Artistic Text Tool. Select paragraph. Paragraph panel. Spacing section. Change value in Leading dropdown. Default is usually a good place to start.

MOVE TO NEXT PAGE

Click right after the text that's before the text you want to move to the next page. Go to Text→Insert→Break→Frame Break to move the text to the next frame or →Page Break to move to next page.

ORPHANS REMOVE AUTOMATICALLY

Paragraph panel. Flow Options. Check box for Prevent Orphaned First Lines.

SIZE

Artistic Text Tool. Select text. Top menu, left-hand side. Font Size dropdown. Choose size or type in size.

Or select text and go to Character panel and use the Font Size dropdown at top.

SMALL CAPS

See *All Caps or Small Caps.*

TRACKING

Artistic Text Tool. Select text. Character panel. Positioning and Transform section. Second option in the left-hand column, Tracking. Click arrow for dropdown menu. Choose desired change.

UNDERLINE

Artistic Text Tool. Select text. Ctrl + U or click on the underlined U in top menu.

Or go to Character panel and choose one of the underlined U options from the Decorations section.

WEIGHT

Artistic Text Tool. Select text. Top menu, left-hand side. Font Style dropdown. Choose from available weights for that font.

Or select text and go to Character panel Font Style dropdown at top.

WIDOWS REMOVE AUTOMATICALLY

Paragraph panel. Flow Options. Check box for Prevent Widowed Last Lines.

WRAP AROUND IMAGE

Move Tool. Select image. Click on Show Text Wrap Settings option in top menu. In Text Wrap dialogue box choose Wrap Style.

TEXT FLOW

AUTO FLOW

Pages panel. Pages section. Double-click on last page spread in section. Go to right-hand edge of last text frame in workspace. Click on red circle to see red arrow. Hold down shift key and click on red arrow. Affinity will flow the text to as many page spreads as needed using the same master page spread format as the last one.

FROM ONE TEXT FRAME TO ANOTHER (ADD)

Click on blue arrow along the edge of the first text frame. Click on second text frame.

FROM ONE TEXT FRAME TO ANOTHER (REMOVE)

Click on the blue arrow along the edge of the first text frame. Click back onto the first text frame. If arrow is not visible, click on that text frame first.

TEXT FRAME

CHANGE SIZE

Frame Text Tool or Move Tool. Click on text frame or layer for text frame in Layers panel. Use Transform panel to input specific values or use blue circles around perimeter and left-click and drag.

ALIGN OR POSITION

Frame Text Tool or Move Tool. Left-click on text frame and hold as you drag. Look for red and green alignment lines to center or align to other elements in workspace. (Turn on Snapping if there are no red or green lines.)

INSERT

Frame Text Tool. Click and drag in workspace.

TEXT STYLE

APPLY

Artistic Text Tool. Select text. Use dropdown menu at top to apply style. Or go to Text Styles panel and click on desired style. Or use shortcut if one is associated with the style.

BASED ON OTHER STYLE

To base a text style off of another style, first apply the existing text style. Next, make any edits to create the new style. Finally, save as new style.

IMPORTED

If you use the import text style option or are merging two files and it appears, you can choose which text styles to import using the checkbox on the far left. If this is for an import with overlapping text style names click on the Rename To option to bring in the text style but with a new name, click on OK to bring it in with the same name, or choose which of the two styles to keep if there is a conflict identified.

KEYBOARD SHORTCUT

For a new style, add a keyboard shortcut in the Style section of the Create Paragraph Style dialogue box where it says Keyboard Shortcut. (Don't type the description, just use the shortcut when you're clicked into the box.) For an existing style, go to the Text Styles panel, right-click on the style name, Edit [Style Name], and then in the Style section of the Edit Text Style dialogue box, add the keyboard shortcut.

NEW

Artistic Text Tool. Select text. Format text. Style dropdown in top menu. New Style. Give style a name and keyboard shortcut if desired. OK.

UPDATE OR CHANGE

Artistic Text Tool. Select text with style to be updated. Make edits. Click on Update Paragraph Style option to the right of the style dropdown menu in the top menu area.

Or, go to Text Styles panel, right-click on text style name, Edit [Style Name], make edits in Edit Text Style dialogue box, OK.

Index

ABOUT THE AUTHOR

M.L. Humphrey is a self-published author with both fiction and non-fiction titles published under a variety of pen names.

You can reach her at:

mlhumphreywriter@gmail.com

or at

www.mlhumphrey.com

www.ingramcontent.com/pod-product-compliance
Lightning Source LLC
Chambersburg PA
CBHW080555060326
40689CB00021B/4864